# MASSEY HALL

# MASSEY HALL

DAVID MCPHERSON

Foreword by Jann Arden

Publisher: Scott Fraser | Acquiring editor: Kathryn Lane | Editor: Allison Hirst
Cover and interior designer: Laura Boyle
Cover (front and back): Gordon Lightfoot at Massey Hall, summer 2018. Photo by Jag Gundu, courtesy of Massey Hall.
Back flap: David McPherson. Photo by Holly Schnider.
Printer: Friesens

**Library and Archives Canada Cataloguing in Publication**

Title: Massey Hall / David McPherson ; foreword by Jann Arden.
Names: McPherson, David (Music journalist), author. | Arden, Jann, writer of foreword.
Description: Includes bibliographical references and index.
Identifiers: Canadiana (print) 20210240415 | Canadiana (ebook) 20210240814 | ISBN 9781459744998 (softcover) | ISBN 9781459745001 (PDF) | ISBN 9781459745018 (EPUB)
Subjects: LCSH: Massey Hall (Toronto, Ont.)—History. | LCSH: Concerts—Ontario—Toronto—History. | LCSH: Music—Ontario—Toronto—History and criticism.
Classification: LCC ML205.8.T6 M172 2021 | DDC 780.78/713541—dc23

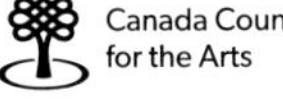

We acknowledge the support of the Canada Council for the Arts and the Ontario Arts Council for our publishing program. We also acknowledge the financial support of the Government of Ontario, through the Ontario Book Publishing Tax Credit and Ontario Creates, and the Government of Canada.



Printed and bound in Canada.

Dundurn Press
1382 Queen Street East
Toronto, Ontario, Canada M4L 1C9
dundurn.com, @dundurnpress

*For Dad: friend, editor extraordinaire, confidante, and concert companion, with whom I've shared some of my favourite Massey Hall memories.*

Playing Massey Hall is like Christmas to me. I'm home; I get to see my family, all my friends. I love the place.

— Gordon Lightfoot

Whether Massey Hall survives through another century or not, its story is already a wonder, a surprise-filled kaleidoscope of Toronto history, and something of a guide to the tastes and passions of North Americans in the twentieth century.

— William Kilbourn, Prologue, *Intimate Grandeur: One Hundred Years at Massey Hall*

# Contents

# FOREWORD

## by Jann Arden

Ask any musician that's been working in the professional music scene in the last sixty years or so where they'd most love to perform in Canada, and I bet you that most of them would say, without hesitation, Massey Hall. The first time I saw my name on the marquee outside its massive brick walls — which are almost cathedral like in stature — I was awestruck. I could not wipe the smile off my face. It was quite unbelievable that I would be standing on the same stage as so many other illustrious singers, songwriters, dancers, poets, actors, philanthropists, orators, politicians, vaudevillians, magicians … and the list goes on. Little old me would be standing out there in the middle of a throng of thousands of souls and singing songs that I'd made up. *So weird.*

There's no other venue like it in Canada. Maybe it's the 127-year history — the ghosts of a long-gone era and all the performers that still long for the spotlight. But you feel something big when you're there. A yearning, a longing, an energy jammed into all the cracks in the walls. All the souls that have sat in those seats for so many decades. The feeling is palpable.

You don't realize until you walk out onto the stage with a full house of excited, grateful people that you are going to be smothered by their presence. Bodies are in front of you, beneath your legs almost, beside you, hanging over the brass railings — hovering over your head like they're dangling from a trapeze. It feels as though there are hundreds of people *on* the stage with you and the band, and they're somehow woven into every single note and every single sound you make. It's a symbiotic experience — everyone joined together with fine gold threads.

It's overwhelming and unforgettable.

On every tour I've ever done, and I've done *a lot* of them, wherever Massey Hall fell on the schedule, it became our big goal: our reward, our gift, of sorts. The whole band and crew were excited to load in and do the shows. I usually had multiple nights booked, so it made it even more special. I think I started most of my tours in the west just so we could finish big in Toronto at Massey — that was the only thing that made any sense. You take your final bow at Massey Hall. I'm hoping that is where I will *indeed* take my final bow. Never too soon to start planning …

I usually stayed in the hotel right across the street, so I would literally walk to work every night through all the folks coming out of Fran's Restaurant. That place was always packed pre- concert with the people who were having a quick bite or a drink. I could hear them talking about me, anticipating the evening. A kind of nervous tension that going to see live shows always generates floated through the air. I felt very voyeuristic listening to bits and pieces of conversations. I *loved* it. Me, with my ball cap and my scarf wrapped about my neck, shooting through the crowd like a pinball — trying my best not to make eye contact with anybody. My road manager, Chris, would hold my hand and we'd march to the stage door filled with purpose. My God, it was so fun.

The "star" dressing room was very charming. Off-white paint covered every corner, radiators and all. It was like walking into a loaf of bread. Familiar and comforting. I think there were what looked like red wine stains on the ceiling, and I'm not kidding. Terrible indoor/outdoor light brown carpeting ran from one corner to the other. It had endured many thousands of spilled drinks, I'm sure. If those walls could talk … The old mirrors were all kind of warped, so I was never sure how good or bad I looked! You couldn't help but think about all the artists that had put on their make-up and given themselves one last glance in those mirrors before they headed out to the cheering crowd. It was magical, despite its obvious fatigue. I was glad to hear Massey was

getting a big splash of love poured over it. It was time for sure.

I could go on forever about this unique place. Massey Hall holds so many brilliant memories for me and so many hundreds of other artists. It's not a building really, it's a person. It feels like a person, a living, breathing thing that has its own personality and its own history and its own family. It's a one-of-a-kind entity, which sounds ridiculous, I know, but it is its *own* deal. You feel it when you walk in and sit down. I've seen many other artists there over the years, and it's always the *best show I've ever seen.*

I had a day off between my Massey shows many years ago, so I was out wandering around. Probably looking for a good coffee or the never-ending quest for a decent meal, and upon returning to my hotel, I made a point of walking in front of Massey Hall so that I could take a photo of my name on the marquee. As I was snapping my tenth pic of the same damn thing, a man in a Blue Jays jersey came up to me and asked if I wanted to buy good tickets for the Jann Arden concert the following night. A scalper was trying to sell me tickets to my own show, and it was spectacular. I asked him if she was any good. He said he didn't actually know who I was but had heard good things.

"How much for the seats?" I asked nervously.

"Two hundred bucks for the pair, but I'll take a good offer."

I ended up buying the seats for my own show, which obviously I will never forget.

They were third row, right smack dab in the middle. I had Chris give them to somebody the next night who was trying to buy tickets *from a scalper*. The shows were sold out — lucky me!

Here's to the next 127 years, Massey Hall. Thank you for making me part of your family.

Jann Arden
June 2021

1894
MASSEY
HALL

# INTRODUCTION

## Massey Hall Forever

Time. That wise marker of the days of our lives. It's the seconds, hours, months, and years that have united all the unique and outstanding performances made, speeches given, and songs sung for the first time on Massey Hall's stage over the past 127 years.

Designated as a heritage building in 1975 under the Ontario Heritage Act and a National Historic Site of Canada in 1981, Massey Hall is one of Toronto's oldest links to our collective cultural past. It has survived when so many other heritage buildings and concert halls in the city have gone the way of the wrecking ball. This iconic building is a symbol of the history, not only of the artists that graced its stage, but of Toronto itself.

The venue recently underwent its first major upgrade in nearly seventy years. This was not simply an exercise in fixing the blemishes of a century-old building. It was a $184 million project that saw the hall close temporarily for only the second time in its history. For more than three years, no crowds gathered

◂ Massey Hall's iconic sign has beckoned music lovers for more than 125 years to enter this temple of music and get lost together for a little while.

The fire escape — a feature of the hall for over one hundred years — was removed during the 2018–21 revitalization.

on the sidewalk outside in anticipation of a show, no performers waited backstage to step out to play for the first time, or the tenth. But with the revitalized hall opening once again in November 2021, years of intermissions now await, new memories will be made, and many more relationships between artist and audience will be forged and developed. Thanks to the vision of current and past leadership, donors, patrons, and all levels of government, my grandchildren's children will have the opportunity to enjoy a show of perhaps some yet-unknown genre in the grandeur of Massey Hall and understand in their own way what makes this place special. The hall that Hart built will continue to be a place "for the people" for at least another century.

Many have called Massey Hall Canada's answer to Carnegie Hall. And the two buildings do share many similarities. Both were built and gifted to their cities by wealthy industrialists (just three years apart) and are woven into the fabric and cultural identities of their cities. And both still stand. But what makes Massey different is that, unlike Carnegie, which has always been a destination for the well-to-do, this is and always has been a blue-collar hall; a gathering place for the entire community, for people from all walks of life and with different tastes and styles. Patrons feel just as comfortable walking through the doors in a three-piece suit as they do in denim and a favourite band T-shirt. Name most any genre, and you'll find that Massey Hall is considered the temple of music in Canada for that group of fans.

"It was a thrill to have all of that sound around you [when I sang with the TSO] ... amazing! That is a great sounding hall when you are on stage."

— Anne Murray, singer

Like a comfortable pair of shoes, or a friend you can always turn to in good times and bad, Massey Hall has been there. When the ushers say it's time, patrons walk through those three red doors, gather with fellow music lovers, sink into their assigned seats, and forget about life for a while. The music envelops the audience, from the orchestra to the upper balcony. It's a collective experience.

So many memories have been made for people over the years. There is the story of a woman going into labour at a concert and refusing to leave until the encore. One woman even named her son Massey because the hall and a Gordon Lightfoot concert played a part in his creation. For anyone who was born and raised in Toronto, who has ever lived here for any stretch of time, or who has made the trip to the city for a performance, Massey Hall is a special place.

As you travel through these pages, take time to savour these special moments in history, to recall and cherish your own Massey memories: your first or favourite show; the first time you heard a particular song; your favourite seat in the house. Then plan a trip to Shuter Street to experience the revitalized hall, generate new memories, perhaps even share the visit with a family member or friend experiencing their first concert at the hallowed hall.

Carnegie Hall (pictured in 1899) opened just three years before Massey Hall.

One wonders if Hart Massey, a strict Methodist and teetotaller, would be rolling over in his grave if he knew they now served alcohol in his Cathedral to the Arts. And imagine if he heard some of the

"It was never a snobby hall ... it couldn't be. People paid what they could pay to come and enjoy the music. You didn't dress up very much ... you didn't see many diamonds in Massey Hall. It was nothing like the Metropolitan Opera House in New York. Massey Hall was not that kind of hall. It was a hall where everybody could go and everybody did go. In some ways, it represented everything that was best about provincial Toronto when it was conceived and that is what Hart Massey would have wished it to be."[1]

— Vincent Massey Tovell, Order of Canada recipient, long-time CBC producer

Gordon Lightfoot waits in the wings of the venue he has played more than any other artist.

acts that have stood on its stage, such as Iron Maiden singing their refrain "666, the number of the beast," with twenty-five hundred fans screaming along. Not to mention the illicit acts of rock 'n' roll excess that have occurred backstage. I like to think he would be pleased and proud to know that his gift to Toronto has become, as well, a gift to the country he loved — one that keeps on giving more than a century after its inception. Sure, the programming has changed to reflect the zeitgeist of each era, but the reality is this: the *raison d'être* of the philanthropist who created the hall — and his mandate that it be a gathering place for the community — is and will continue to be the essence of Massey Hall. Over the years, Hart's act of charity has touched and enriched the lives of generations of Canadians. And, thanks to this recent revitalization, will continue to do so for generations to come.

Massey Hall worshippers gather to sing in 2016 for a Choir! Choir! Choir! show.

The incredible acoustics and intimate ambience at Massey Hall are an audio engineer's dream, the ideal space to capture live performances. From the 1950s to the 2000s, more than a dozen albums were recorded at Massey. I will highlight those that stand out for their unexpectedly high sales, quality, and importance to the artists' careers.[2]

> "I love the earthy simplicity of the wood in Massey Hall. It sings warmly back to you, carrying all the voices that have ever sung there before."
>
> — Feist, singer-songwriter

Asked what makes Massey special, artists unanimously agree on the aforementioned two traits: its intimacy and its acoustics. When you are on that storied stage and set to perform, you feel as if you could hug the audience. It feels that intimate.

For 127 years, the hall has withstood depressions, gentrification, calls for its demolition, and most recently a pandemic. Yet, the Grand Old Lady of Shuter Street still stands, a beacon of hope and guardian of the arts.

Massey Hall forever.

# CHAPTER 1

## The House That Hart Built

During the late 1800s, churches dominated the Toronto skyline. The tallest structure was the newly constructed seven-storey Beard Building located at 163 King Street East. Public transit was in its infancy, and most residents navigated the city on horse-drawn streetcars, or by foot or bicycle. Electricity arrived in Toronto in the 1880s and the tracks for the electric streetcar were just starting to be laid throughout the city. The population of Toronto was exploding, jumping from 86,400 in 1881 to 181,200 by the time Massey Hall opened in 1894. Queen's Park and the Ontario legislature had opened the previous year (1893). The Gooderham and Worts distillery was in full operation and was the world's largest whisky distillery. The same year Massey Hall opened, the *Toronto Mail* and the *Toronto Empire* merged to create the *Mail and Empire*, which later became the *Globe and Mail*. The *Evening Star*, the precursor to the *Toronto Star*, was also just a few

◂ Massey Hall's interior basked in sunlight during the early 1900s.

From the 1870s to the 1890s, Toronto was a city of churches, and the Metropolitan Methodist Church (known today as the Metropolitan United Church) was where Hart Massey and his family worshipped.

months old. This is the life and times industrialist Hart Massey experienced.

Since churches dominated the cityscape, and Massey was a devout Methodist, it's not surprising these religious pillars became the architectural inspiration for the design of his proposed music hall.

On a cool autumn evening in 1892, Hart Almerrin Massey, in the course of an after-dinner conversation, asked a matter-of-fact question of his guest and good friend Frederick Torrington, the organist of the Metropolitan Methodist Church. "Torrington, what do you think of the corner of Shuter and Victoria as a site for a music hall?" The pair was together at Massey's mansion, Euclid Hall, at the corner of Jarvis and Wellesley streets (a building that still stands today as the Keg Mansion). Torrington was likely surprised but intrigued by this proposition and was highly supportive.

At the time, Toronto did not have a large public hall for mass meetings or music festivals, which were usually held in one of the city's arenas or churches. One of the only venues for large-scale events was St. Lawrence Hall, which had opened in 1850. Named for Canada's patron saint, the hall was for many years the centre of cultural and political life in Toronto, hosting balls, receptions, concerts, exhibitions, lectures, and performances by the Toronto Vocal Music Society and the Toronto Philharmonic Society. But by the 1870s, with a growing population, the thousand-seat venue was proving insufficient for larger gatherings.

As a philanthropist, Massey felt the city deserved a grander place, one that could host up to three thousand people and "which shall be of the greatest benefit to the greatest number of the citizens of Toronto."[1]

MUSIC FOR THE PEOPLE.

HONEST MECHANIC (Musically inclined)—"This here 'cheap music,' Johnnie, is a trifle too gay for us; I guess we kin stay home and play the mouth-organ."

"A place for the people" was the guiding principle of Hart Massey's gift to the city; while this cartoon pokes fun at that notion, over the years the venue has proven it is a place for everyone.

The securing of property rights and the first plans for the building, which was to be named the Massey Music Hall, were a family secret. Hart Massey had purchased the parcel of land at Shuter and Victoria streets, and Torrington was the first person outside his inner circle to hear of Massey's grand plans for a building that would be "for the people." Hart's vision for the new hall was to provide high-calibre entertainment at minimal cost to a broad spectrum of Toronto's citizens.

The building would also serve as a living memorial to Hart's eldest son, Charles, who had died in 1884 of typhoid fever at the age of thirty-six. Charles had loved music, and as a young man had been the church organist.

It wasn't long before these private Euclid Hall conversations were shared more broadly

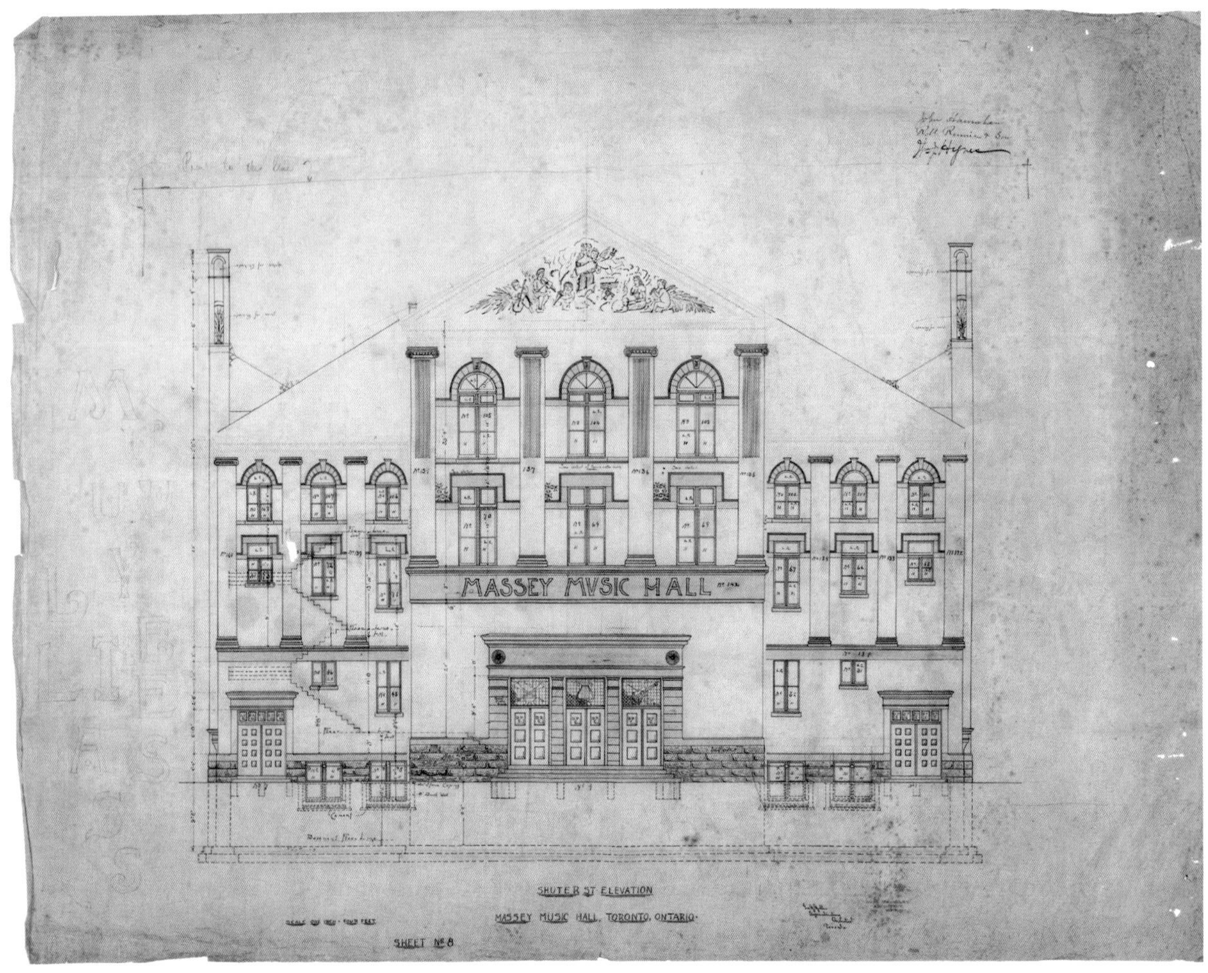


Sidney Rose Badgley's architectural drawing of the hall's facade from 1893.

with civic leaders, and the idea edged closer to reality. The management of and financial arrangements for Massey Hall were defined as part of a gift to the city. For the sum of one dollar, Massey and his wife, Eliza Ann Massey (née Phelps), transferred the property to his friend John J. Withrow[2] (a politician, businessman, and philanthropist) and two of their sons: Chester Daniel Massey and Walter Edward Hart Massey, who would serve as the first trustees. The three men were given complete control, with the right to appoint assistants, but they could not at any time mortgage or otherwise encumber the property. These terms would apply to any subsequent trustees.

To Massey, the idea of expressing his philanthropy in terms of architecture was not a new one. The remodelling of a Methodist church at Newcastle (the family's original home) and the church that the Masseys attended during their years in Cleveland, Ohio (1870–82), and alterations made to several Toronto churches already bore witness to his interest in donating to public buildings.[3]

Massey selected Sidney Rose Badgley, an Ontario architect who had moved to Cleveland, Ohio, in 1887, as the lead designer for his new music hall. Badgley was a prolific church architect at the time, especially of Methodist churches.[4] One of the finest examples of his church design is the Pilgrim Congregational Church in Cleveland, completed in 1894, now a National Historic Site. This was the first church building in America built to function as both a church and a community-service centre.

Massey saw Badgley as "a bright, well-trained, pliable young Methodist who would cheerfully take close direction (or should we call it interference?) more readily than one of Toronto's established architects."[5] Massey spent hours reviewing and revising plans for the hall. During construction, he worked closely with Badgley, personally overseeing the smallest details.

Euclid Hall, the Massey family home on Jarvis Street, still exists today as a Keg restaurant.

As author Andrea Yu writes in "Massey Hall: Past, Present and Proposed Future,"

> Badgley was inspired by Methodist church architecture; he gave Massey Music Hall a U-shaped interior with a vaulted ceiling. As the "exotic" Moorish Revival style was considered popular at the time (spreading even to Hart Massey's private mansion on nearby Jarvis Street), Badgley designed the hall's interior similar to the Alhambra Castle in Granada, Spain, with Moorish arches, fireplaces, and horseshoe-shaped galleries. The vaulted, beamed, and decorated plaster ceilings with scalloped

MASSEY MUSIC HALL

*Dated June 5th, 1894*

H. A. MASSEY, et al

—AND—

J. J. WITHROW, et al

Deed of Trust

WATSON, SMOKE & McMASTER

The Deed of Indenture between Hart Massey and the City of Toronto.

arches and cusps are a few examples of the hall's Moorish design.[6]

On the building's facade, Massey preferred a simple neo-classical look with Palladian arches.

On April 20, 1893, the permit for the proposed hall was issued, following approval from the city commissioner. Work on the building progressed quickly, with the nearby Don Valley Brick Works supplying all the bricks for the new building. Five months later, on September 2, six-year-old Vincent Massey — Hart's favourite grandson — laid the cornerstone for the building. By December, three of the eight-ton iron trusses for the roof were already in place.

The cost of building Massey's great hall would eventually balloon to more than $150,000, far more than the $60,000 reported in the *Globe* the day after the permit was granted.[7]

On June 14, 1894, a capacity crowd attended the opening concert at the new Massey Music Hall — a performance of Handel's *Messiah*. An aging and ill Hart presented the keys to the building to the mayor of Toronto, Warring Kennedy, and shared his hopes for the future of the venue with the sell-out crowd:

> "Massey Hall is hallowed ground. It has vibes like the old Ryman Auditorium in Nashville. It's that kind of place. I remember the first time I stood on the edge of that stage doing sound check, I was in awe. I said to myself, 'this must be some mistake, I don't belong here.'"
>
> — Murray McLauchlan, singer-songwriter

> I express the hope that the trustees will have the fullest confidence of the public, and that the people of Toronto and surrounding country will give them their hearty cooperation in using the property to cultivate and promote an interest in music, education, temperance, philanthropy and religion, and in every way to make the most out of this building for the good of the people in whose midst it stands.[8]

Today, Massey's generous gift remains a reflection of city life and an essential cultural hub. It continues to give the greatest benefit to the greatest number of people, not just from Toronto, but from across Canada.

Industrialist, philanthropist, teetotaller, Methodist, patron of the arts — these are just a few of the adjectives that can be attributed to Hart Almerrin Massey. To understand how the iconic building at 178 Victoria Street went from an idea in Hart's head to a Canadian cultural institution, it's important to understand the man behind the vision.

As an entrepreneur, Massey had amassed a fortune. Like many self-made millionaires, in his later years, he allocated time and money to philanthropic pursuits, financing iconic permanent monuments such

Massey Music Hall program for opening night 1894.

as Massey Hall, Hart House, and the Fred Victor Mission.

Daniel Massey (Hart's father) was left in charge of the family farm while his own father fought in the War of 1812. With no paternal tutelage, the teenager became independent. By necessity, a strong work ethic flourished in him, a trait his eldest son, Hart, inherited. Daniel left home before he was twenty-one and became both a farmer and an entrepreneur, building a successful business manufacturing farm machinery. Hart was born in a log cabin in Haldimand Township, Upper Canada, on April 29, 1823. From an early age, Daniel's eldest son showed similar ambitions to those of his father; he also inherited his strong moral beliefs. By the age of fifteen, Hart was organizing religious services in the family home. This led to lifelong service to the Methodist church. His values centred on God, hard work, and community service. Pierre Berton captures the young Massey's strong work ethic and his transformation from farm hand to industrialist: "At seven young Hart was hauling water. At twelve he was marketing crops. At sixteen he was a foreman of a lumber gang. At twenty-one he had taken over his father's fledgling sickle-and-cradle business and, before he was through, had fashioned it into an international industrial empire."[9]

Hart was educated locally as well as in Watertown, New York, where he had relatives. Between 1842 and 1846, he attended Victoria College in Cobourg, Ontario. The year 1847 was a milestone one for Hart. In January, he received title to the family homestead, and five months later he married a young American girl, Eliza Ann Phelps, who shared his values. The newly married couple settled in Haldimand, where they would remain for years and raise a family of four boys and one girl. Quickly, Massey became a community leader. He served as a school trustee, magistrate, and member of the local reform association. Hart also helped erect a new church and served as Sunday school superintendent. He continued to act as a magistrate, and in 1861 was appointed coroner of the United Counties of Northumberland and Durham. A freemason, he joined Durham Lodge No. 66 in 1866, becoming a master mason eleven years later. He also became head of the Newcastle Woollen Manufacturing Company.[10]

In 1847, Daniel also opened a foundry near Newcastle, Ontario, and within five years became its superintendent. Then, on January 17, 1853, Hart and his father formed a partnership: H.A. Massey and Company. Between 1851 and 1861, Hart followed rapid American technological developments with calculated interest, returning from trips to New York State with a series of production rights — for a mower, a reaper, a combined reaper and mower, and a self-raking reaper — that would enhance the reputation of the Massey foundry. In February 1856, nine months before Daniel Massey's death, the partnership was dissolved and Hart became sole proprietor of the business with Daniel's strong financial backing in the form of interest-free notes totalling £3,475. Under Hart's aggressive direction, the foundry flourished.[11]

In the early 1860s, Massey expanded the business using advertising, marketing, and mass publicity as key sales tools. He published his first illustrated catalogue, which showed the medal awarded for his threshing machines in 1860 by the Board of Arts and Manufactures of Lower Canada. In March 1864, fire destroyed the Newcastle works at a loss of $13,500, but it didn't take Hart long to rebuild the plant to meet the increasing orders for his innovative farm implements. In 1867 his combined reaper and mower, sent by the Board of Agriculture of Upper Canada to the international exposition in France, won a medal, and the company's first European orders followed.

In 1870, Hart incorporated the Massey Manufacturing Company, which was relocated to Toronto in 1879 and expanded significantly with the purchase of the Toronto Reaper and Mower Company, and Massey directed the firm's successful entry into foreign markets; in fact, it was the first North American firm of its kind to go abroad. In 1891 he merged A. Harris, Son and Company Ltd., and other Canadian rivals to form Massey-Harris Company Ltd., of which he was president until his death in 1896.[12] Massey Manufacturing Company Works (a new plant) was built in Toronto and opened in 1882. Located on King Street West, it was the largest plant in the city at the time. Eventually, the Works included reading rooms, game rooms, and a small lecture hall for the use of employees and community residents, since most employees lived nearby. Soon a library, a glee club, an orchestra, and various sports teams

The Massey Manufacturing factory, known as the Works, located on King Street West in downtown Toronto, employed nearly a thousand people at its peak.

Hart Massey and his family, late 1800s.

flourished there, too. By 1890, the plant employed nearly a thousand workers.[13]

Hart and Eliza Ann settled on Jarvis Street in 1882 in a property he later named Euclid Hall.[14] A Puritan and pious man, Massey did not allow cards, dancing, alcohol, or tobacco in his home.[15] Pierre Berton describes a typical morning for Hart during his years living at Euclid Hall:

> Hart Almerrin Massey was a gaunt towering figure in silk hat and frock coat who made punctuality a fetish and philanthropy a duty. Promptly at 6 a.m., come sleet, rain or storm, he flung wide the door of his home and plucked the morning *Globe* from the mat. Once when a newsboy was late he stood out in the elements for twenty minutes in gown and slippers to reprimand him, then sent his coachman over with a new winter outfit for the ragged lad. Promptly at 9:15 his carriage deposited him at the sprawling Massey works on King Street.[16]

But in 1884, tragedy struck. Hart's son Charles died of typhoid fever at the age of thirty-six. Charles had been a great lover of music and had founded the Massey Silver Cornet Band, the Massey String Orchestra, and the Massey Glee Club. Hart may never have fully recovered from the shock of losing his eldest son and company leader at such a young age. After all, Charles had been the driving force behind the company's rapid expansion and success.

This heartbreak was followed six years later by the death of Hart's youngest son, Fred Victor, who died in April 1890 at just twenty-two. These tragedies hit Hart hard. As a coping mechanism, the industrialist turned his attention more than ever to philanthropy, investing in everything from education to health care. As William Kilbourn writes, "He had always regarded himself as accountable to God for his talents and his fortune, and his own Methodist congregation adopted as one of its rules a specific prohibition against 'laying up treasure on earth.'"[17]

Two of the treasured gifts Hart bestowed on the City of Toronto were Massey Hall and the Fred Victor Mission. The music hall was a tribute to Charles's love of music; the mission was a monument to honour Hart's youngest son. "Each memorial was an attempt to express in physical form the interests, abilities, and personalities of his sons. It seemed as if their deaths triggered within Hart a desire to share his financial success with others through long-standing functional buildings. He had always been a man motivated by duty."[18]

Massey Hall view from the gallery in 1894.

In the fall of 1895, Hart suffered a stroke from which he never fully recovered, and he never left his house after January 1896. Massey died at Euclid Hall on February 20, 1896 — his grandson's ninth birthday. At Massey Music Hall that night, Haydn's *The Creation* was being performed under the auspices of the Trades and Labour Council. At the end of the performance, the conductor announced Massey's passing, whereupon the "Dead March" from Handel's *Saul* was reverently performed.

The successful businessman and entrepreneur left behind an estate that totalled more than $2 million (about $41 million in today's money).

Hart Massey is buried in Toronto's famous Mount Pleasant Cemetery.

MASSEY
HALL
HALL

# CHAPTER 2

## The Early Years: Opening Night to the Great Depression

During its first year, Massey Music Hall attracted 357,000 people to a wide variety of performances that included orchestras, opera singers, and evangelists. As William Kilbourn writes in *Intimate Grandeur*, "In its prime, Massey Hall was the most important building in the city."[1]

In the early years, choral and classical music were frequent offerings at Massey Hall. Two organizations — the Toronto Mendelssohn Choir (TMC) and the Toronto Symphony Orchestra (TSO) — first on their own, and later together, were staples that drew capacity crowds and formed part of a regular subscription series of highly anticipated concerts each season.

The TMC was born the same year Massey Music Hall opened (1894). The following year, on January 15, choirmaster Augustus Vogt led this group of

◄ The hall's iconic neon sign beckons patrons to enter through the three red doors.

(left) The interior of Massey Hall, showing what it looked like shortly after opening in 1894.

(right) A *Globe* advertisement from October 10, 1933.

like-minded choral singers in its inaugural concert at the hall. After studying at the New England Conservatory in Boston and the Leipzig Conservatory in Germany, Vogt returned to Canada in 1889, becoming conductor of the Jarvis Street Baptist Church choir. Over the next five years, he led its transformation into the TMC. The origins of the choir were rooted in Toronto's church music tradition.

Vogt thought the acoustics of Massey were "ideal for the acapella work he wished to conduct."[2] He, along with his committee, bargained with the hall's trustees to book the hall for a January date in 1895 at a reduced price of forty dollars.[3] Named after famous Leipzig composer Jakob Ludwig Felix Mendelssohn, the Toronto Mendelssohn Choir was composed of 167 members (sixty-six sopranos, forty contraltos, twenty-six tenors, and thirty-five basses) at this inaugural concert. Approximately 1,800 people attended the performance, including Lieutenant Governor George Kirkpatrick and Lord Mayor Warring Kennedy.[4]

After briefly disbanding the original TMC in 1897, Vogt assembled a new choir with new rules — requiring all members to submit to a voice and reading test every season and also to arrive at rehearsals with a lead pencil and their parts thoroughly mastered.[5] It wasn't long after the debut of this choir that Vogt envisioned pairing his singing group with a major symphony orchestra. The first of these collaborative concerts occurred in February 1902 when the TMC played with the Pittsburgh Orchestra under Victor Herbert. In subsequent years, trips to New York's Carnegie Hall and other cities in the United States and Canada followed as the reputation of Vogt's choir grew. The annual performances of Handel's *Messiah* became a TMC tradition that Torontonians looked forward to each December.

From the moment the doors opened in 1894, and continuing to the present day, authors, celebrities, and dignitaries have employed their voice in this historic building.

Hart Massey desired his hall to be a place for people from all walks of life to experience a variety of forms of entertainment *and* education. Religious mass meetings, by all denominations, were frequent in the hall's early days. One of the first of these, in the fall of 1894, was a series of revivals led by Mr. Dwight Moody. The American evangelist conducted spiritual awakening work over the course of several weeks and many meetings. Numerous conversions were made. According to the *Globe*, for most of these revivals, the building was "packed to suffocation."[6]

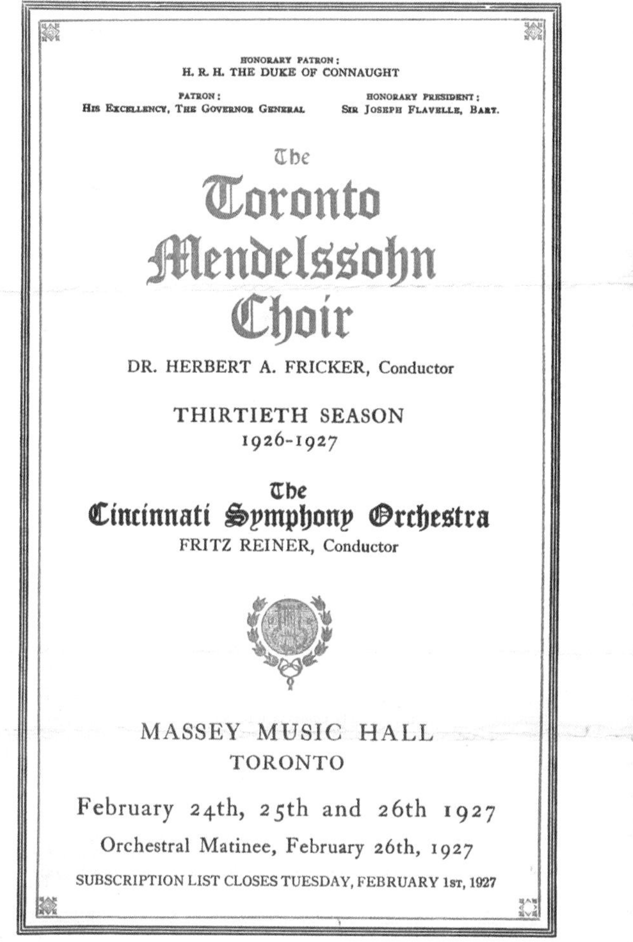
HONORARY PATRON:
H. R. H. THE DUKE OF CONNAUGHT
PATRON:
HIS EXCELLENCY, THE GOVERNOR GENERAL
HONORARY PRESIDENT:
SIR JOSEPH FLAVELLE, BART.

The Toronto Mendelssohn Choir

DR. HERBERT A. FRICKER, Conductor

THIRTIETH SEASON
1926-1927

The Cincinnati Symphony Orchestra
FRITZ REINER, Conductor

MASSEY MUSIC HALL
TORONTO

February 24th, 25th and 26th 1927
Orchestral Matinee, February 26th, 1927
SUBSCRIPTION LIST CLOSES TUESDAY, FEBRUARY 1ST, 1927

A 1927 program for the Toronto Mendelssohn Choir, one of the earliest regular performers at Massey Hall.

"I've always loved it because it had such a historic significance to the City of Toronto. It was the gathering place for everything whether it was political meetings, union meetings, community meetings, musical presentations ... it became part of the fabric of the city ... the focal point for downtown Toronto."

— Riley O'Connor, chair, Live Nation Canada

Author Sir Arthur Conan Doyle, best known for his mystery novels featuring Sherlock Holmes, was one of the earliest writers to lecture from Massey Hall's stage. Billed as "Readings and Reminiscences," his appearance was described as "an opportunity that may not occur again," according to an article in *Toronto World* on November 14, 1894. On a lecture tour of North America, the author had already appeared in Boston and New York before arriving in Toronto to speak on November 26. Reserved seats were priced at fifty and seventy-five cents, and 1,500 people attended.[7] Conan Doyle spoke for ninety minutes about his childhood and the genesis of his famed character, Holmes. He also read from some of his novels. He ended the evening reading some passages from a yet unpublished work, *The Lord of Chateau Noir*, which made a deep impression on the audience. "The first encouraging criticism ever published on my work came from a Toronto journal," said Conan Doyle. "I forget the name of it, but it was on my novel *Micah Clarke*."

Since Massey abstained from alcohol, the temperance movement was another common topic of discussion in his public hall. One of the first speakers to broach the subject was Lady Henry Somerset, who lectured specifically about Women's Temperance in 1895. Over the ensuing decades, the Women's Christian Temperance Union and other, mainly religious, groups held similar mass meetings.

On December 29, 1900, Winston Churchill arrived in Toronto to give a lecture at Massey Hall entitled "The War as I Saw It." The British war correspondent and author (who would later become one of Britain's most famous prime ministers) spoke about his experiences during the Boer War (1899–1902). "Every seat in the vast hall was occupied, every person present anticipated an enjoyable evening, and no one was disappointed."[8] The evening ended with the audience singing "God Save the Queen."

Two years later, author, orator, and educator Booker T. Washington spoke to a crowd of more than two thousand men and women from all walks of life on questions of race in his lecture "The Negro and His Future."[9] Between 1895 and 1915, Washington was the most influential spokesperson for Black Americans. On this night, he spoke about the birth of the Tuskegee Institute (the industrial school for Black students for which he was the first president) in Alabama and how education was the best solution for the advancement of his people. At the conclusion of the lecture, the audience joined together in singing "God Save the King."[10]

From Massey Hall's early years, its stage was often used as a pulpit for politicians who rallied their party faithful into a fervour during election campaigns or addressed the populace on the pressing subjects of the day. Massey Hall never played favourites. From conservatives to communists, all political parties were welcome. In October 1904, future Canadian prime minister Sir Wilfrid Laurier gave a powerful patriotic speech. The headline in the *Toronto Daily Star* the next day read "Laurier Captures Queen City's Heart."

"I tell you that the nineteenth century has been the century of American development," he thundered. "Let me tell you that all the signs point this way, that the twentieth century shall be the century of Canada and Canadian development. For the next seventy years, nay for the next one hundred years, Canada shall be the star towards which all men who love progress and freedom shall come."[11]



Franco-German contralto and international opera star Sigrid Onégin brought her heavenly voice to Massey Hall in 1930.

• • •

Paul Robeson, an American bass baritone singer, actor, and activist, performed at Massey Hall in 1931.

From the early 1900s, when the venue was less than a decade old, until the arrival of automobiles, Toronto's streets were filled with another kind of traffic. With more than 7,400 horses living and working in the city by 1891, the presence of these animals was an integral part of urban life. Most were work animals used for delivering a variety of products from businesses such as groceries, butcher shops, and dairies. Doctors also used horses to make house calls and police and firefighters fulfilled their civic duties using equine power. The well-to-do, like the Masseys, owned carriages, while the majority of the population reached their destinations each day riding on horse-drawn streetcars. Looking back today at black-and-white photographs of this era, one may conclude it was an idyllic time, without the pollution, noise, and congestion of our modern age. The reality is, however, that the age of horse transportation was not perfect. Jammed into busy streets not unlike our urban gridlocked ones, the animals also produced noise, waste, and a potential danger to passersby if startled.[12]

Imagine it's late afternoon, circa 1901. The last rays of sunlight filter through the beautiful stained-glass windows scattered throughout Massey Hall. You are an audience member settled into your seat ready to enjoy the incredible acoustics of the hall and listen to a symphony performance. As the conductor leads the musicians into the second movement, you strain to hear each note, but the muffled sounds of the clip-clop, clip-clop of horses on Shuter Street interferes with your experience, preventing you from appreciating the subtle sounds of the first violin or the whisper of the woodwinds.

Even though the facade of the brick building was soundproofed, the single-pane stained-glass windows did little to stop both sound and light from entering the space. Not wanting to compromise the hall's acoustics, and to allow for performances during the day when natural light would not interfere with the act on stage, temporarily blind one of the patrons, or alter the mood the show required, one of the first changes to Massey Hall occurred in the early 1900s when the approximately one hundred exterior and interior stained-glass windows were boarded up. A dozen of these windows facing the street featured pictures of classical composers such as Bach, Beethoven, Handel, and Chopin. The Faircloth Brothers in Toronto had fabricated these ornate windows during the 1890s. Their shop was located directly across from Massey Hall, on the northeast corner of Shuter and Victoria. After the windows were covered, Massey Hall remained relatively untouched for the next three decades. The only other additions occurred in 1911, when fire escapes were added for extra safety, and in 1917, when the Albert Building behind the hall was added to the structure and later converted into a backstage area.

Prior to the formation of Toronto's official symphony orchestra, other travelling orchestras (such as the Boston Symphony and New York Philharmonic) visited Massey Hall, often performing with the TMC. After a few false starts to launch a full-time symphony for Toronto, in 1922 the seeds of the New Symphony Orchestra were planted. Rehearsals, led by conductor Luigi von Kunits, were held in the basement of Massey Hall. The first concert of the New Symphony Orchestra (later renamed the Toronto Symphony Orchestra or TSO) took place there on April 23, 1923. Ticket prices ranged from twenty-five to seventy-five cents; players received $3.95 each for the performance. William Kilbourn captures the atmosphere of this inaugural performance in his book *Intimate Grandeur*:

> As the young musicians turned up onstage, the 25-cent seats in Massey Hall's upper gallery filled rapidly. A respectable smattering of 75-cent and 50-cent ticket holders occupied the lower gallery and ground floor. The maestro strode in swiftly, chestnut mane flowing, bowed grandly to their welcome, and tackled the overture of *Der Freischutz* and the rest of the short programme to mounting excitement and applause.[13]

In his history of the TSO, *Begins with the Oboe*, Richard S. Warren also describes this inaugural performance:

> The principal oboe played an A and the orchestra tuned. Then Dr. Von Kunits stepped onto the podium, raised his baton, gave the downbeat, and they were away into the Overture to *Der Freischutz* by Carl Maria von Weber. The remainder of the program consisted of a *Slavonic Dance* by Antonin Dvorak, two *Hungarian Dances* by Johannes Brahms, and the Symphony No. 5 in E minor by Pyotr Il'yich Tchaikovsky.[14]

The next day the press raved about the new orchestra and the conductor, and two more concerts were planned and presented the following month. The roots for the TSO were now planted. In 1923/24, the size of orchestra ranged from sixty-five to seventy-five, and they held twilight concerts bi-weekly on Tuesdays. All of the players had regular day jobs and came to play at Massey Hall during their dinner break.[15] Von Kunits's symphony became popular, and these concerts were highlights of the Massey Hall season. "The twilight concerts proved a boon to young audiences and performers alike, and were a promising omen for the future of music in Toronto," wrote Kilbourn.[16] Each year, new programs were added to the orchestra's season, such as a children's concert jointly sponsored by the Toronto Board of Education and the Toronto Catholic School Board, which was held on a Saturday morning.

"It's warm ... the sound is so warm in that place though it's a big hall and it's high up, the top floor is still close to you when you're performing. Acoustically, it's just so wonderful. All the great names loved Massey Hall. They loved its sound. It wasn't, in that way, the most luxurious hall, but it had this beautiful, warm sound."

— Vincent Massey Tovell, Order of Canada recipient, long-time CBC producer

During the 1927/28 season, the New Symphony Orchestra officially became the Toronto Symphony Orchestra (TSO); thus began nearly six decades where Massey and the TSO were partners, until Roy Thomson Hall opened in 1982. One other highlight of the TSO at Massey Hall as the 1920s came to a close was its first radio broadcast across Canada on the CNR Radio Network (1929).[17] "This first broadcast was not only a momentous occasion for the orchestra but also an important step for Canadian radio, and it marked the beginning of the TSO's long association with this media."[18]

Another notable concert by the TMC at Massey Hall took place February 1915, when they held a free concert for the troops of the Second Canadian Contingent.

Despite its original name, Massey Music Hall, Toronto's most cherished venue has hosted an amazing array of events throughout its history: from horticultural exhibitions and boxing matches to royalty visits, beauty pageants, and typing contests. One of the biggest bookings, besides concerts, were speeches. Evangelists raised the roof with religious conversion sermons. Teetotallers espoused the virtues of temperance. Women gathered to discuss the suffragette movement. Labour unions held closed-door meetings. Every major political party held rallies inside the building's four walls. Mother Teresa held crowds spellbound with her stories a pair of times at Massey Hall. Even the fourteenth Dalai Lama, the Tibetan spiritual leader and Nobel Peace Prize winner, shared his message of compassion from the stage in 1990.

"At one point, it was certainly Toronto's most important building as a place of community rather than commerce," author William Kilbourn told the *Globe and Mail* on the occasion of the hall's centennial in 1994. "All the great people of the twentieth century who went on speaking tours came through Massey Hall. It's quite incredible. Toronto was just about the number one location on a lot of touring circuits, and without Massey Hall, it wouldn't have been as easy to come here."[19]

On January 9, 1914, Helen Keller brought to Massey Hall a "moving message from the world of darkness." A *Globe* reporter wrote, "Rarely does one find an audience keyed to such intense sympathy as that which filled Massey Hall last evening to hear and see this wonder among mankind." Many blind people were in the audience and to them she exclaimed, "I greet you all, my comrades in the dark!" Keller was accompanied to the stage by her teacher, Mrs. Anne Macy (better known today as Anne Sullivan), who gave the main address of the night, telling her pupil's remarkable story of how she was born deaf and visually impaired, but eventually learned how to speak. At the end of the evening, Keller spoke and answered several questions from the audience. When asked if she liked Toronto, she replied: "The rain came and spoiled my

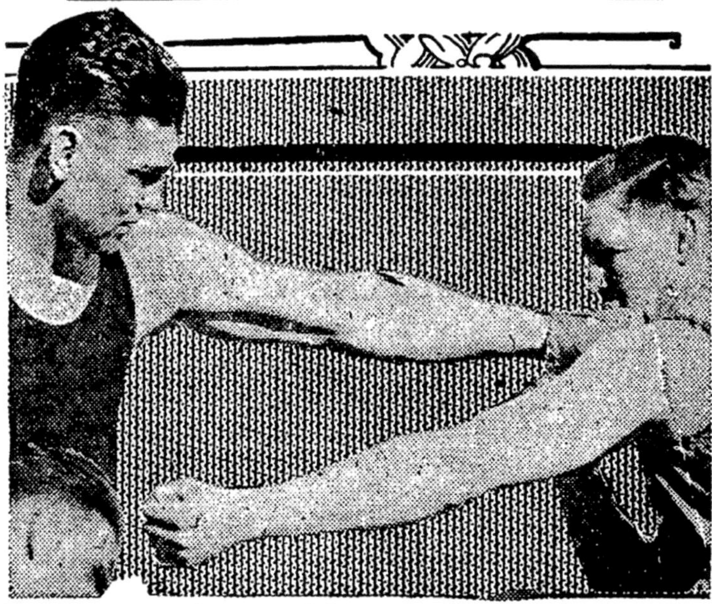

25 THE TORONTO DAILY STAR, FRIDAY, SEPTEMBER 19, 1919.

AMUSEMENTS. AMUSEMENTS.

BOXING

G. A. C.

MASSEY HALL

TO-NIGHT AT 8.30

Band in attendance. Plan on sale, Moodey's, Spalding's and Massey Hall.

JFH

In the early 1920s, boxing matches were held regularly at Massey Hall, as this ad from the *Toronto Daily Star* shows from September 19, 1919.

visit. I haven't seen the city, but I love the people."[20]

On March 9, 1923, Lottie Betts Tushingham entered Massey Hall to compete in the annual Canadian typewriting championships. Three thousand spectators filled the hall to watch the speed and accuracy at which her fingers moved from key to key. Reaching a top speed of ninety-nine words per minute netted her the winner's silver cup. During nearly two decades of competing in speed-typing contests, the Ottawa-born Tushingham became an international star. By the time she retired from competition in 1928, she had won the competition eighteen times.[21] Years later, Canadian literary critic Northrop Frye won a similar typing contest on the same stage.

Boxing and wrestling were other non-musical offerings held frequently at Massey Hall during its first fifty years. From 1919 to 1921, these sports out-rented all other forms of entertainment at the hall by three to one. The ring was usually placed in the middle of the stage. All levels of boxing matches were presented at Massey, from the Canadian Amateur Athletic Union championships to professional title bouts and exhibition matches to raise money for charities. One of the most famous pugilistic displays occurred on April 12, 1919, when Jack Dempsey, shortly before winning the world heavyweight championship, refereed preliminary bouts onstage at Massey Hall and sparred in an exhibition match.

One of the first jazz performances at the hall took place on October 1, 1924, when Paul Whiteman, who the media dubbed "The King of Jazz," brought his "army of jazzmen" to the Massey crowds, captivating his adoring fans. As a *Globe* reviewer wrote of Whiteman's music, it "alternatively galvanized and amused, teased and exhilarated."[22]

Back in 1908, Enrico Caruso, the acclaimed Italian operatic singer and one of the first global celebrities, had come to Toronto for the first time, performing at Massey Hall.

When Caruso returned to play the hall in 1920, it was the most expensive ticket for a single artist that year in Toronto. In fact, it broke all previous box office receipts at the venue up until that point. The sold-out show included an extra hundred seats on the stage. Ticket prices ranged from four to seven dollars. Unofficially, the papers reported the box office receipts came to about eighteen thousand dollars. Following the show, Caruso went out onto the fire escape and sang to the throngs gathered on Shuter Street below who could not afford a ticket to the show.[23]

• • •

(top) The Italian opera star Enrico Caruso first played Massey Hall in 1908. By the time he returned in 1920, the ticket sales for his appearance broke all previous box office records.

(bottom) A program for a three day Royal Music Festival that was held in 1901 to mark the visit of the Duke and Duchess of Cornwall and York to Toronto.

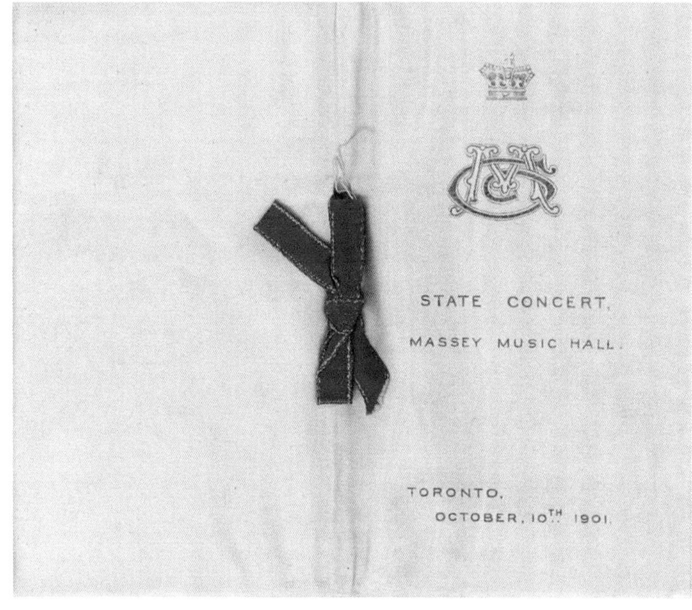

A signed photo from Lenora Sparkes, a British American mezzo-soprano, who performed at Massey Hall in November 1920.

The first signs of "trouble" for Massey Hall showed up even before the Great Depression of the 1930s. In the 1926–27 fiscal year the concert hall ran at a deficit — the first since the early part of the war years. This shortfall signalled that operating costs from ongoing maintenance were adding up. Repairs to the hall were constantly required to maintain safe operation of the lighting, plumbing, heating, electric systems, roof, ceiling, seats, walls, stairways, and fire escapes. The cost of fire insurance was also increasing at this time. Most years, any surplus the hall made was allocated to pay for these improvements and upkeep. Competition from other venues also took away community business that once came to the hall. For example, the large meeting bookings started to shrink as other spaces such as the Royal York Hotel (1929) opened up for these public gatherings.[24]

The Great Depression of the 1930s left millions unemployed in Canada. In *Toronto Since 1918: An Illustrated History*, James Lemon provides some startling statistics: in 1931, 17 percent of Torontonians were unemployed. Two years later, the census reported that 30 percent were not able to find work, and in 1935, 25 percent of the population in the city and the suburbs were on relief. For most, during the Depression years, a night out at Massey Hall was a luxury they could ill afford, resulting in fewer bookings. For those who were not hit as hard by the financial collapse, the arts remained an important social activity for their mental health. Massey Hall played a role in helping these families cope, providing a temporary escape from the hopelessness surrounding them.

Deficits, the economy, fewer full nights at the hall, and increasing maintenance costs led to the first conversations about the possibility of selling the building. In 1929, a real estate consortium expressed interest in purchasing the site. Vincent Massey spoke at a special board meeting that December about the "general style and type of building he would like to see erected in case these negotiations [led] to an actual sale of the property."[25] After discussions with the consortium's representative, the trustees decided to offer the building and the site for the sum of $650,000. No agreement was reached. Conversations about selling the hall ceased until 1931, when an agent of British cinema interests met with trustees to discuss a possible purchase. Nothing came of these discussions either, but they were the impetus for major renovations that were undertaken in 1933, thanks to a generous gift from the Massey Foundation, which contributed all the funds needed to modernize the building and enhance the concert-going experience for patrons.[26]

MASSE
HALL

# CHAPTER 3

## The Jazz Age and Beyond

Buildings must withstand recessions. Buildings must also overcome and rise above competition from newer, more modern concert halls. The story of Massey Hall's survival shares similarities with other heritage properties throughout North America. It is a story linked to the political climates and economic realities of each decade the hall has stood at the corner of Victoria and Shuter streets. To survive 127 years, a building needs luck and passionate citizens who champion heritage property preservation and these landmarks' value as not just physical structures, but cultural institutions. Passion and luck alone are not always enough to withstand the wrecking ball. Throughout its lifespan, from the moment the first stone is laid, any landmark, no matter how treasured by its citizens, experiences periods where its fate is questioned.

Major renovations were made to the building in 1933, with the wife of the late Vincent Massey, Alice Parkin Massey, directly involved in the process. The

◂ A young crowd eagerly files into Massey Hall to see a visiting orchestra in 1947.

American Jazz singer Sarah Vaughan first stepped onto Massey Hall's stage on April 19, 1948, as part of a Jazz at the Philharmonic concert that also featured saxophonist Charlie Parker.

original seating capacity of 3,500, which had occasionally been increased to 4,000 by using part of the stage, was reduced to 2,765. Six rows of seats in the lower gallery were removed to create a smoking lounge. Rows of seats at the back of the main floor orchestra were also removed to allow for the remodelling of the front lobby to make the entranceway more spacious and inviting. The lobby was refurbished in an Art Deco style and enhanced with a diamond pattern marble terrazzo floor.

When the hall reopened, one of the key features that patrons noticed as they walked into the building was a large ornate clock, which had originally hung in the Parliament Buildings of Upper Canada and later in the Queen's Hotel, located on the north side of Front Street (the current site of the Royal York Hotel), until its demolition. Six feet across and heavily gilded, it's surrounded by a red-and-gold crown in which a lion on one side and a unicorn on the other are fighting. A rose, a thistle, and a shamrock are entwined along the bottom of the clock with the motto *"Dieu et Mon Droit"* — "God and My Right."[1] Wide, shallow-stepped stone and steel staircases also replaced the steep, rickety, flammable wood staircases that had led to the galleries. The building's red-and-black motif exterior, now synonymous with Massey Hall, was also introduced. Originally, the colour of the exterior of the building had been more sombre, with not much adornment, much like a church. Inside, red-and-gold wall decoration was added, along with a grey-green ceiling and stylish shaded lamps. For the first time, the original solid wood seats were replaced. Patrons were amazed by the transformation. As one of these attendees exclaimed, "The Grand Old Lady of Shuter Street is a debutante once more!" These extensive renovations cost more than $40,000 (about $800,000 today) and, as part of the Massey Foundation contribution, an outstanding loan of eight thousand dollars and all overdue interest payments were forgiven, so, upon reopening, the management started afresh, debt-free.[2]

• • •

The 1930s at Massey Hall was a decade filled with classical performances — most by the TSO and also many by a variety of visiting orchestras. During the 1931/32 season, Ernest MacMillan was appointed as conductor of the TSO.[3] Changes and additions included adding concerts for schools, which started at 4:15 p.m. so classes would not be disrupted. The following season, the top ticket prices increased from seventy-five cents to $2.50 to help pay for the orchestra members, which now numbered ninety musicians.[4] MacMillan would lead the orchestra for the next twenty-five years.

The Toronto Mendelssohn Choir performed in 1942 when Herbert Fricker (the second conductor of the TMC) gave his farewell concert, choosing his favourite work, Bach's Mass in B Minor.

Crowds of Salvationists pack the house to listen to General Evangeline Booth speak. The daughter of the Salvation Army's founder made the historic visit to Massey Hall in 1935.

A key literary talk given at Massey Hall during this time was by acclaimed German novelist Thomas Mann, who spoke there in 1938. On November 2, 1939, William Patrick Hitler, nephew of Adolf Hitler, gave a talk entitled "What the German People Are Thinking." The twenty-eight-year-old arrived in the United States on March 31 of

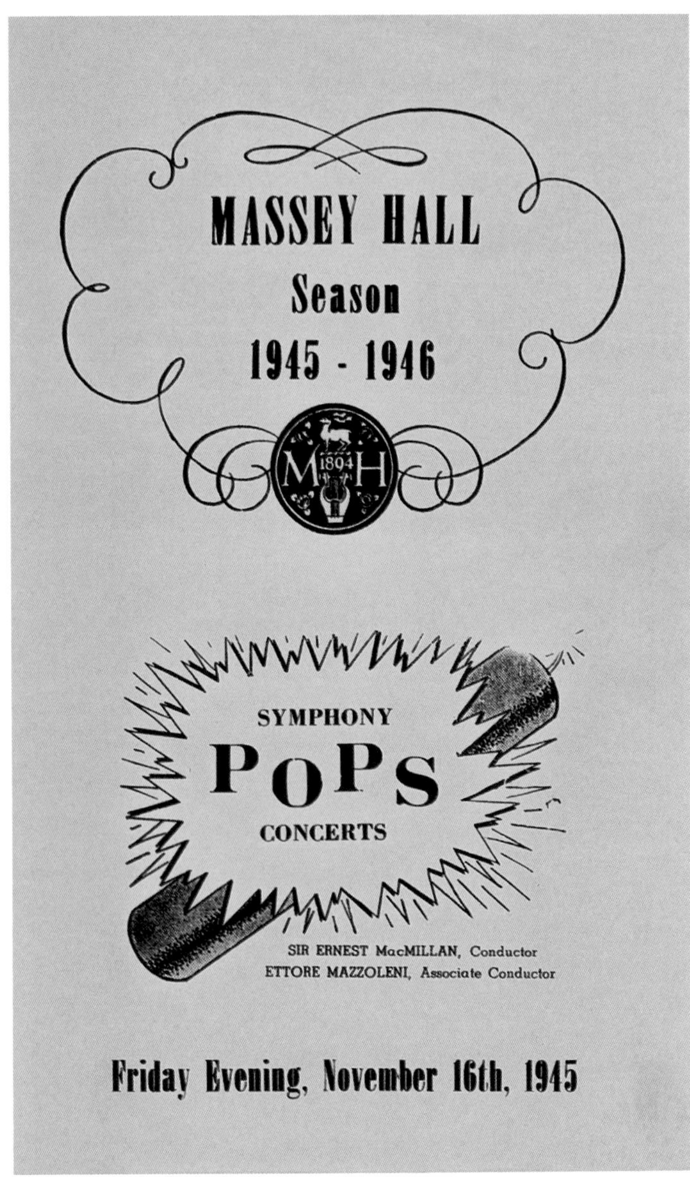


Sir Ernest MacMillan, who conducted the TSO for twenty-five years from 1931 to 1956, introduced the "Pops" concerts, which combined classical and popular music.

that year to begin a North American speaking tour. William's father was the half brother of the Nazi leader. Although William was born in Liverpool, he had visited his uncle in Germany in the early 1930s. While working there at a bank, he slowly started to despise the Nazi system with its racial and religious persecutions as he learned more about it and watched his uncle's lust for power grow.

In stark opposition to such political content, comedy also featured prominently and frequently at Massey Hall, from early variety shows to stand-up comic performances. Over the years, the hall has hosted a who's who of comedic geniuses. While there were sporadic comedic moments throughout the venue's first half-century, it really took hold starting in 1943. As part of a war bond event, Victor Borge, the Danish musical monologist entertained the Massey audiences with his skits, stories, musical mixups, and satires twice in a matter of months.

Jazzman Paul Whiteman, like many artists today, was not happy when his star power grew too large for Massey. By 1938, Whiteman's appeal and audience had grown to where he could fill Maple Leaf Gardens. He missed the Old Dame. The headline from the October 10, 1938, edition of the *Globe and Mail* encapsulates his longing to return to his beloved hall on Shuter Street. "Hockey Arena Not 'The

"There's an intimacy to the venue, even at a backstage level, that you don't normally feel at other theatres."

— Riley O'Connor, chair, Live Nation Canada

Tops' to Whiteman: King of Jazz Looks Lonely in Vast Oval — Prefers Massey Hall." Whiteman preferred the acoustics of Massey and, of course, the venue's intimacy. "Personally, I couldn't stand listening to a band in one of those arenas," he told the reporter before his Gardens show.[5]

George Gershwin, the legendary American composer, who penned popular songs for both stage and screen — creating many tunes that are now considered standards — also dabbled in jazz. On January 19, 1934, he appeared at Massey Hall as a piano soloist, playing his *Rhapsody in Blue* and *Concerto in F*.

On March 7, 1946, twenty-year-old Canadian jazz pianist Oscar Peterson, who hailed from Montreal, made his first of many appearances at Massey Hall. An ad for the show proclaimed, "Now in Toronto. Canada's Sensational 20-Year-Old Piano Stylist Modern and Classical Programme (with rhythm accompaniment)."[6] Fans could purchase tickets at the King Edward Hotel or at Massey Hall's box office. Prices ranged from ninety cents up to $2.40. The *Globe and Mail* headline the following day proclaimed, "Swing Pianist Stirs Massey Hall Throng." Reviewer Dillon O'Leary wrote, "Oscar Peterson's first appearance in Massey Hall last night had the large audience shouting for encores as he left, and revealed a swing pianist of wide abilities and a young man with a promising career."

Toronto music lovers were fortunate to catch George Gershwin at the hall in 1934, as he died at the height of his career just three-and-a-half years later.

Glenn Gould played Massey Hall numerous times during the fifties and sixties, and debuted at just fifteen years old in 1947.

Peterson's set included "mainly standard tunes of bygone years, which have weathered the test of time."[7] Following this successful debut, Peterson returned to Massey the following year. The popular pianist would go on to play Massey four more times over the course of his long and distinguished career. A contemporary of Peterson's, eccentric

"The life of Massey Hall has included so many divergent themes that only the untiring composer, Time, could unite them in one unfinished symphony."
– S.M. Creighton, author of *The Story of Massey Hall*

musical genius Glenn Gould made his debut at Massey Hall two months later; the teenage pianist performed with his school and the Toronto Conservatory Symphony Orchestra as part of their annual closing concert. Gould made his first professional concerto debut the following year, at age fifteen, with a pair of performances on January 14 and 15, 1947. With Bernard Heinze conducting the TSO, Gould played Beethoven's Piano Concerto No. 4.

On May 19, 1949, jazz trumpeter Louis Armstrong packed Massey Hall, and to glowing reviews. Alex Barris raved in the *Globe* the next day, "Old Satchmo himself — aided no end by his five fine friends — made the rafters rock as he trucked out his Sunday-best jazz, flavoured with just the right amount of expert showmanship."[8]

• • •

The next facelift to the Shuter Street shrine occurred during the postwar boom. In 1948, the oak flooring on the main level was replaced as the wood was deteriorating and creaky. Fire concerns about a building made entirely of wood (think of the Notre Dame Cathedral fire in April 2019) were also a factor in the decision to install a new stage, now mounted on sleepers — wood blocks randomly distributed to reduce resonance that causes feedback — between the stage surface and the new poured concrete base. This would be the largest renovation until the 2018 remaking. Several design changes were made, including new paint in places to better blend the hall's original Moorish influence with the Art Deco elements added in 1933. During this renovation, the seats on the main floor were replaced to include a sliding mechanism that was typical of movie theatres of the day.

On September 28, 1949, the TSO opened the newly refurbished hall with a performance of Beethoven's *The Consecration of the House*, written for a similar occasion in Vienna many years ago. As the *Globe and Mail* remarked the next day, "The comfort of the new seats and the peace of mind occasioned by the fireproofing have undoubtedly enhanced the public's enjoyment of the music."[9]

Trumpeter Louis Armstrong, one of the most influential jazz artists of the twentieth century, first played Massey Hall in 1949.

The Second World War years brought a couple more trials for the venue and its management. The global conflict touched all aspects of people's lives. No different than the Depression years a decade earlier, leisure activities such as enjoying a musical or other performance at Massey Hall was a welcome escape for many, and kept the hall busy. Still, the structure needed constant attention. In 1944, suggestions surfaced once again from local politicians claiming it was time to build a new hall. During this time, a *Globe and Mail* article stated, "Erection of a new Massey Hall is the post-war project dearest to the heart of Ald. Harold Fishleigh who spent the past month talking to prominent people who might lend their assistance." The alderman believed the hall was outdated and needed replacing. The Massey Foundation contemplated the idea and Toronto architect A.S. Mathers even prepared preliminary plans for a new Massey Hall. After the war ended, this project did not go any further.[10]

The postwar economic boom brought yet another significant renovation in 1948, which is covered in the next chapter, quieting any further talk of building a new hall. Despite these investments, in the ensuing decade the venue continued to show its age. In 1955, a large chunk of plaster fell from the ceiling — luckily while the hall was empty — and the entire ceiling was reinforced with a strong wire mesh to hold it in place. These Band-Aid solutions staved off the wrecking ball despite constant calls from politicians and citizens to construct a more modern facility.

Following the war years, the next two decades in Canada were a time of economic prosperity and stability. In the 1950s and 1960s, Jazz at the Philharmonic, a touring group of contemporary jazz musicians led by impresario Norman Granz, played Massey Hall a couple of times a year. A few key literary talks were given at Massey Hall during the decade, including Nobel Prize for Literature winner William Faulkner in 1953. This would be the last time a literary event was held at the hall until thirty-four years later, when the Toronto International Festival of Authors brought in Canadian author Robertson Davies, along with American playwright Arthur Miller and British author Anthony Burgess, for a sold-out literary event that saw scalpers selling tickets outside for as much as fifty dollars.[11]

"All Quiet at Massey Hall as Toronto Reds Mourn," proclaimed the headline in the *Globe and Mail* on March 10, 1953. The night before, nearly two thousand people crowded into the hall to "mourn the passing of Joseph Stalin, hear Russian songs and listen to speeches by leading Canadian

A crowd winds around the block waiting to attend a rally at Massey Hall for MP and Conservative party leader George Drew on June 23, 1949.

Communists."[12] The affair was invitation-only. Toronto police were on guard outside in case of any protests, but there were no demonstrations. On the stage that night stood a red and black draped easel with a large photograph of the dead Russian leader. During the evening, three choirs — the Jewish Folk Choir, the Russian-Canadian Women's and Youth's Choir, and the Shevchenko Male Chorus — performed a variety of Russian songs. The night opened with the Canadian national anthem, followed by the Russian national anthem. City, provincial, and federal leaders all decried this meeting of Canadian communists as "an instance of disloyalty to the Western World."

On April 25, 1957, Progressive Conservative leader John Diefenbaker launched his national campaign for prime minister at Massey Hall.

A crowd of Lester B. Pearson supporters gather outside Massey Hall on March 22, 1958, during the federal election campaign.

On Tuesday, May 19, 1955, after a day spent in Montreal as a guest of the United Nations Association of Canada, the former United States First Lady Eleanor Roosevelt arrived for more meetings in Toronto, capped off by an evening address at Massey Hall, which was filled to the topmost gallery. Trailblazer Helen Boorman Tucker, a mother, teacher, and peace advocate from Mississauga, arranged the speaking engagement and introduced Roosevelt.[13] In her newspaper column "My Day," the former First Lady summarized her visit: "The people in Toronto were most kind in their welcome and it gave me a sense of warmth to be there."[14] Roosevelt, who was a UN delegate, spoke about universal human rights.

In 1957, comedian Victor Borge returned to the Massey Hall stage, after having played other venues such as Maple Leaf Gardens and Toronto's Casino Theatre, located at 87 Queen Street West, which opened April 13, 1936, and offered three films a day as well as burlesque shows.[15]

The phrase "the greatest" is packed with hyperbole. Pizza parlours love to lay claim that their pies are the "world's greatest." In the realm of popular music, critics debate annually what are the greatest records. Entering this debate is a jazz concert at Massey Hall on May 15, 1953, that many critics today consider "the greatest jazz concert ever." At the time, it was just another Friday night and only six hundred of a possible 2,700 seats had been sold.

What made it memorable in the annals of history is that for one night — and one night only — five of the universally acknowledged greatest jazz cats of the bebop tradition played together, sharing the stage for a loose and spontaneous forty-seven-minute set that consisted of only six tunes and part of a seventh. This all-star quintet, who author Mark Miller describes as "a bop fan's dream band," included alto saxophonist Charlie Parker, trumpeter Dizzy Gillespie, pianist Bud Powell, bassist Charles Mingus, and drummer Max Roach.[16]

But how did this all-star band come together? Organized by Dick Wattam and the New Jazz Society, the quintet was a wish list of players to stage a concert. Magically, they all agreed to play, each for a different price, ranging from $150 (Mingus and Roach) to $500 (Powell). The total cost for these five legendary jazzmen: $1,450. Since ticket sales didn't cover the New Jazz Society's expenses, some of the musicians left Toronto without seeing a dime. Only Parker, Powell, and Roach were eventually paid in full,

General Wilfred Kitching conducts at the annual Salvation Army Congress on October 18, 1954.

## Ted Heath with Stan Kenton's orchestra, April 1956

Ted Heath, considered one of England's greatest postwar big band leaders, made his North American debut in 1956 – conducting Stan Kenton's orchestra.[17] In a unique musical exchange program, Kenton, a popular American bandleader and arranger, travelled England on tour, while Heath performed in the U.S. Heath's tour was drawing to a close and, by some minor miracle as there were no Canadian dates listed on their itinerary, the band showed up at Massey Hall. Fred Augerman was there. He recalls this incredible performance.

> Our family insurance agent heard on the radio that Heath the band were to appear at Massey. Knowing what a big band freak I was, he called my mother and asked if he could take me and a friend to see the show. There we were, front-row centre balcony, with a complete unobstructed view of that wonderful stage. My friend Bob Priddy, who was the only other sixteen-year-old I knew who was into jazz, along with our chaperone, were ready and waiting for the 7.30 p.m. performance. Nobody expected that tickets would sell as quickly as they did because Ted Heath was not yet a household name in Southern Ontario. But, thanks to jazz radio shows in the region like Joe Rico (*Jump For Joe*) in Buffalo and Byng Whittaker (*Bing's Choice*) in Toronto, who both played a lot of Heath, the demand was so great for tickets a second show at 10.30 p.m. was added and it also sold out.
>
> At 7.40 p.m., Phil MacKellar, a local jazz DJ, appeared and apologized for the delay. McKellar said the band's uniforms had just arrived from the cleaners and they would appear shortly. And appear they did! You could have cut your finger on the crease on their pants; the blue blazers with a British crest they wore were also immaculate. You were almost blinded when the

spotlights shone on their instruments … they were just gleaming. The band blew Massey apart for the next hour and a half. When they concluded, they received a five-minute standing ovation, with shouts of "Encore. Encore!" Unfortunately, because of the late start, there was no encore since the audience for the second show was anxiously waiting its turn to see this magnificent orchestra.

At the late Murray Patterson's "Rendezvous 2000," one of the finest Kenton tribute presentations I've ever attended, I had the pleasure of meeting Don Lusher, the Ted Heath lead trombonist for many years. I asked him, "Back in 1956 on that first tour of the States, do you recall playing in Toronto?" Without hesitation, he said, "You mean Massey Hall? That was the second-best concert of the entire tour, with the exception of Carnegie Hall on May 1."

while Mingus received the master tapes of the concert recording in lieu of payment. Gillespie was not paid at all, and later described that the cheque he was handed on that May night in Toronto "bounced, and bounced, and bounced like a rubber ball."[18]

This now-legendary Massey Hall show was the first — and only — time these five brilliant musicians performed together. Within two years, Parker, who was already in poor health at this show, would be dead.

A major factor in the lack of ticket sales to the concert was that promoter Wattam decided not to advertise it. Word of mouth alone, he figured, would put bums in the seats.

Don Brown was twenty years old when he sat in the balcony at Massey Hall to watch the show. Reminiscing, he told *Toronto Star* writer Geoff Pevere in July 2011, "I'm sure people didn't know about it." Brown said the fact Wattam decided not to advertise was ridiculous. "When Norman Granz brought Jazz at the Philharmonic to Massey Hall every September, he bought full-page ads in the *Star*, the *Telegram*, and the *Globe and Mail* … [but] Wattam said, 'No no no no. Word of mouth. Word of mouth. It'll be mentioned on the radio and everybody will run down to buy tickets.'"[19]

Another possible reason for the lack of ticket sales was the fact that a heavyweight boxing title bout in the Windy City, at Chicago Stadium, was happening on the same night. Most of North America was

**Jazz Festival**

**DIZZY GILLESPIE • CHARLIE PARKER**
**BUD POWELL • MAX ROACH**
**• CHARLES MINGUS**
***Plus***
**CBC All-Stars • 17-Piece Orch. led by Graham Topping**
**MASSEY HALL—TONIGHT—8:30 P.M.**
**Tickets NOW at all agencies and Premier Radio**

A poster from 1953 advertising what later became known as "The Greatest Jazz Concert Ever."

glued to their TV sets and radios to witness the rematch between heavyweights Rocky Marciano and Jersey Joe Walcott. The first fight between the two had been an epic battle, and fight fans expected the same from this bout. In fact, Dizzy Gillespie seemed more interested in the fight than in playing his trumpet and snuck out the side door during an extended intermission to watch the fight and toss back double scotches at the Silver Rail across the street. He had to practically be dragged back from the bar to play.

Charles Mingus was frustrated by Dizzy's antics (he was always known as a bit of a clown) and just wanted to get on with the music. In the end, the fight's outcome was underwhelming, and Marciano easily defended his title. A left hook and an uppercut, two minutes and twenty-five seconds into the fight, left Walcott stunned and flat on his back in the ring, unable to stand up before the count of ten.

The *Globe and Mail*'s Alex Barris was lukewarm in his concert review the next day, and described the show as "a two-and-a-half-hour clambake," summarizing it as follows: "All in all, it was neither a great concert nor a bad one."[20]

Years later, drummer Max Roach recalled the atmosphere at this concert as pretty difficult. "The people in that dressing room and the issues and problems they had, it would need a whole conference of psychologists to work it all out," he said. "It was

On May 15, 1953, for the first — and only — time, Charles Mingus, Charlie Parker (shown here on saxophone), Max Roach (shown on drums), Dizzie Gillespie (shown on trumpet), and Bud Powell performed together.

pure spontaneity. That's the thing about that date. We just went on the stage, and things began to happen."[21] The quintet did not have any time to rehearse; and Mingus played everything by ear. In an interview with Bill King in 1992, Roach revealed that while the quintet had worked together in smaller versions before in various musical settings, they had never before all been on the same stage until that night at Massey Hall. "We were considered at that time the young Turks. We were a new group of young musicians on the scene, so to speak. Charles Mingus got involved because Oscar Pettiford broke his arm in a softball game while working with Woody Herman. Pettiford was our first choice. We were happy Mingus came in because we had formed a record company and wanted to record."[22]

The reality is this: it was likely a brilliant PR man, an expert on spin, who much later coined the phrase *The Greatest Jazz Concert Ever*. The first live recording of this evening, when Mingus took the tapes (recorded off the house PA) and released it on his Debut label on three ten-inch LPs in 1956, was entitled *Jazz at Massey Hall* by the Quintet. Charlie Parker could not be listed on the original album cover for contractual reasons and was billed as "Charlie Chan," an allusion to the fictional detective and to Parker's wife Chan. Later, Fantasy Records bought the tapes and issued most of the concert on a single twelve-inch LP. The descriptor *greatest* was not affixed to the concert until eighteen years later when, in 1973, the recording was re-released by Prestige Records, adding the title "The Greatest Jazz Concert Ever."

But what really went down at this so-called "greatest jazz concert ever?" Jack Batten, the crime novelist and long-time arts reporter for the *Globe and Mail* and other Toronto papers, attended the legendary performance. When he was a teenager, jazz was the music that tugged at Batten's heart. CBC Radio had a weekly program called *Jazz Unlimited*, and Batten tuned in every Saturday afternoon. During those formative years, the writer also went to a variety of Toronto venues to listen to live jazz. Those regular visits continued into the 1960s. "To hear jazz in Toronto, you went to clubs like the Colonial Tavern or the Town Tavern; both of those places booked everybody," Batten recalls. "The problem is, you were sitting in a noisy milieu. Going to Massey Hall was such a treat — to hear music with great acoustics and everybody was there just for the music." Or, as critic David Lee puts it, "Jazz in a jazz club is a night out, jazz at Massey Hall is a bit of a pilgrimage." Lee further notes that the Massey Hall concert thus helped to affirm bebop's validity as sophisticated music and the quintet's legitimacy as serious musicians, worthy of performing beneath its hallowed proscenium arch.[23]

LIVE AT MASSEY HALL

## The Quintet, *Jazz at Massey Hall*, 1956, Debut Records

*Rolling Stone* named it one of the fifty Greatest Live Albums of All Time. In the original liner notes, Bill Coss, editor of *Jazz Today*, said, "Asides aside, they blew music of startling quality that night. This album commemorates no zenith of a style but it is eloquent music played by five exceptional musicians, something of a distinction among jazz recording circles as a general rule."

Batten joined the New Jazz Society a couple of months before "The Greatest Jazz Concert Ever" arrived at Massey. He was not involved with the planning and describes Wattam as a "bit of an autocrat." No matter what others suggested, he did it his way.

The inspiration for this show was a successful concert the Society had held previously at a union hall in the city's west end: the Lennie Tristano Quintet. "Wattam thought he could have an even bigger success to have these five guys," Batten recalls. "Musically, it was, but the show only drew about half the hall."

Batten describes the concert as tremendous. "Bud Powell had a set to himself with the local rhythm section; that, to me, was the highlight of the evening. A big band of young Toronto musicians, modern bebop guys, played too. The reason? There was a union regulation at the time that whenever anybody from the U.S. played a concert at Massey Hall, you had to have a standby by a Canadian band. They didn't have to play, they just had to be there."

From 1973 onward, the first time the concert was released with the "Greatest Jazz Concert Ever" tag, the mythology surrounding this show has continued to grow. As the calendar flipped on another decade at the hall, the venue bid adieu to the 1950s with a TSO performance of *A Midsummer Night's Dream*. The decade to come was a tumultuous one for Massey; it was also one of new beginnings. The call for a new home for its primary tenant (the TSO) grew louder as the inadequacies of the aging building started to show. On the booking side, the folk-music movement found a home with groups like the Weavers, Peter, Paul and Mary, and Canada's own Ian & Sylvia taking the stage.

- 11th Concert Season -

International Artists

presents

GLENN GOULD

Pianist

MASSEY HALL, TORONTO

MONDAY EVENING, NOVEMBER 11th, 1957

A program for the young genius Glenn Gould's concert in 1957.

STAGE →

STAGE
LEFT

EXIT

# CHAPTER 4

## For Folk's Sake: The 1960s

The late 1960s to the late 1970s is considered the darkest and most uncertain period in Massey Hall's history. As William Kilbourn writes in *Intimate Grandeur*, "By the late 1960s, the building's flaws, to many musicians who used it and to those in charge of its fate, appeared irreparable."[1] Again, competition from new venues added to the demolition debate and further made the case that its lease on life was coming to an end. The O'Keefe Centre, designed by architect Peter Dickinson, opened in the city in 1960, bringing "a new sophistication and glamour to Toronto's theatre-going experience."[2] By 1963, the Royal Alexandra Theatre on King Street, which had opened in 1907, was only operational a few weeks each year and was facing the wrecking ball before local businessman Ed Mirvish bought it and invested the money to restore the historic theatre.[3] The modern O'Keefe Centre, combined with the Royal Alex's

◂ An artist's view of the hall, from stage left.

"Massey Hall is legendary for a reason. I can still recall noticing the patina on the wooden stage when I was eighteen years old, my first time. There is a magic there that is palpable."

— Serena Ryder, singer-songwriter

renovations, highlighted just how dated Massey Hall had become.

This trend of heritage buildings in North America on death's door due to deterioration and competition is not unique to Toronto. Starting in the mid-1950s, with the announcement of the construction of the Lincoln Center for the Performing Arts in New York City, the future of Carnegie Hall (which opened three years before Massey Hall, in 1891) was in doubt. Deals were struck to sell the building to developers who planned to demolish it and erect a forty-four-storey office tower on the site. The deal fell through, but as the Lincoln Center neared completion, and with Carnegie's biggest tenant (the New York Philharmonic) set to move to the new facility, the date of March 31, 1960, was set for the historic hall's demolition. Fortunately, on May 16, as a result of special state legislation, New York City purchased Carnegie Hall for $5 million, and a new non-profit organization called the Carnegie Hall Corporation was chartered.[4]

With Massey Hall's future in serious doubt, in 1967, Edward Pickering, TSO president at the time, hired an American consultant, who submitted a report on all aspects of the TSO's future. One of the major findings and recommendations was that the symphony needed a new building. William Severns, the music hall consultant, said, "I urge you … not to waste time and money on makeshift facilities, that all efforts be directed toward planning, financing, and constructing a fine new auditorium."[5]

Massey Hall trustees commissioned a study of their own. The Toronto engineering firm they hired also recommended that the board seek to build a new concert hall. The board did not rule out demolition of the old hall, but never made a formal decision.[6] It wasn't long before the media reported these studies. On October 13, 1967, a *Globe and Mail* headline proclaimed, "Home of the Great Massey Hall Doomed." The story outlined details of how the building would be sold and a new Massey Hall would be built elsewhere. In the daily papers, the corridors of City Hall, and in the public, talk favouring the need for a new hall — one that contained modern amenities and was better suited for the TSO — increased. Even Governor General Vincent Massey, the grandson of Hart Massey who had laid the first stone back in 1894, had this to say in 1967, shortly before his death: "The Grand Old Lady of Shuter Street has served Toronto well for over seventy years. But she has had her day."[7]

As the new decade began, these debates persisted. As the future of Massey Hall remained uncertain, periodically there were more offers to purchase the building. In 1970, Edward Pickering, now co-chair of the Massey Hall Committee, made the following prediction: "No architect has actually set a date on the life of Massey Hall, but it seems we've got about five years before a great deal of money will have to be poured into the building for major structural repairs."[8] Following Pickering's statement, talks over the next two years quickly turned, on the suggestion of the Massey Hall Committee, to consider disposing of Massey Hall once and for all. The thinking was this: sell the building and the half-acre site for the approximately one million dollars it was

The bass section at a Toronto Symphony Orchestra rehearsal in 1963.

appraised at and use the money as a contribution toward building a new hall.

The talk of building a "new" Massey Hall (initially proposed to open in 1976 at Front and Simcoe) was first mentioned as early as 1967 when Pickering, then president of the TSO, and Hugh Lawson, chair of the Massey Hall Board of Trustees, announced the plan. The board was evenly divided. Some members felt Massey Hall should be preserved even after the new Hall was built and that there was room in the city for both venues. Others agreed that demolishing the old building and selling the land was the only option. International consultants sought out for their opinion on the debate ruled out renovation, saying it would be too costly and there was no room for expansion on the site. All aspects of the building were "obsolete," they said.

Rumours continued to run rampant as politicians, consultants, real estate developers, and concerned citizens debated whether Massey Hall had indeed reached the end of its life. The heritage group Time and Place called a meeting on November 9, 1972, to discuss Massey Hall's future. At this gathering, Edward Pickering aimed to dispel rumours that a decision had been made as to the venue's fate. There had been offers and inquiries to purchase the building, he assured them, but no decision had been made. At the end of the day, the meeting was inconclusive. The future of the venue was still unclear. Fortunate for preservationists such as the Time and Place group, the 1972 municipal election on December 4 that year ushered in a new city council committed to historic preservation. The City of Toronto instructed the Massey board to continue to operate the old building as a condition of being helped with the planned new hall.[9] In 1973, the City of Toronto named Massey Hall a heritage site, publicly acknowledging the property's value to the community. This designation helped halt any further conversations about selling or demolishing the building.

Debates over Massey Hall's fate continued in the media, behind closed doors, in office buildings, and in the coffee shops of the city throughout the 1970s — rising and falling in intensity like waves battering a sea wall. What drove these discussions? Emotions? Passion? Politics? The question always came back to the amount of money necessary to renovate and keep Massey Hall safe from the wrecking ball versus investing that money into a brand-new modern facility. Until the most recent revitalization campaign, frequent facelifts are what truly saved the hall from demolition and guaranteed its future.

While debates about Massey Hall's future raged on outside the hallowed halls, the music never ceased. The 1960s is a decade defined not only by the rise in popularity of rock 'n' roll, but also of the folk movement. Singer-songwriters and storytellers spread the gospel of free love and folk music from Yorkville Avenue in Toronto to Bleecker Street in Greenwich Village, New York. Yorkville was home to one of North America's most vibrant folk scenes. Years before the area became the bourgeois blocks we know today, marked by celebrity sightings and Coach purses, it was a music mecca. Hippies and youngsters congregated nightly in the area's bars and coffee houses to chat, commune, and worship emerging folk legends that included Joni Mitchell, James Taylor, Ian & Sylvia, Gordon Lightfoot, and many others who got their starts playing small clubs like the Purple Onion, the Riverboat, and the Penny Farthing. As Bernie Fiedler, owner of the Riverboat, who still promotes Lightfoot's shows across Canada today, recalls, "You could barely walk down the street it was so crowded with people."

This generation were one of the first to rebel from their parents' values. Disenchanted by the politics of the day, these youth were driven to create their own cultural revolution with a matching soundtrack. The songs of the day spoke to this growing disenchantment, with lyrics laced with political statements and social commentary. Pete Seeger — revered today as one of the pioneers of the folk music revival — played Massey Hall on February 20, 1960, and was a regular there throughout the decade. The Weavers were another of the first folk groups to perform at Massey Hall and bring their political songs to the storied stage. The American folk quartet, which formed in Greenwich Village, made their Massey debut three months after Seeger's inaugural performance on May 6, 1960.

Bob Dylan famously summed up the sentiments of this generation in "The Times They Are a-Changin'," his anthem and title track of his 1964 album. Artists such as Dylan (who made his Massey Hall debut November 13, 1964), Phil Ochs, Peter, Paul and Mary, Joan Baez, and Canadians Joni Mitchell and Gordon Lightfoot honed their sounds in clubs in Greenwich Village and Yorkville before their popularity grew and they could pack the concert halls. Singer-songwriter Murray McLauchlan remembers his inaugural Massey moment — not as a performer, but as a fan:

> The first time I ever went into that hall was to see Bob Dylan. I saved, stole, and cajoled money from my brother to buy a ticket. Dylan was still a folk

A boisterous crowd of many races and faiths gathered in Massey Hall to protest against apartheid in South Africa and raise funds to help those facing racial discrimination in Canada.

singer at that point. My big memory of that moment was sitting in the balcony, in the cheap seats, and Dylan had not said a word for the entire concert. He's up there on stage, in a suede jacket and suede boots, and he's playing all these amazing songs … all the protest songs like "The Lonesome Death of Hattie Carroll" and "With God on Our Side." I'm there to worship at the temple. Then, he mumbles, "Here's something new I just wrote, and haven't really played it anywhere," and proceeds to sing "Mr. Tambourine

Man." I could not get that song out of my head for the rest of that winter. I wasn't even sure of the words, but it just stuck in my head.

In the 1960s, folk singers found a welcome home at Massey Hall. Pete Seeger, one of the pioneers of early protest songs, was one of the first to perform there.

Out west, in the Haight-Ashbury district of San Francisco, a more psychedelic music movement took root as sounds evolved from folk to folk-rock to even more progressive explorations with bands such as the Grateful Dead and Jefferson Airplane. No matter the label — folk or psychedelic rock — at the root of all these musical movements was a new-found independence of this generation of teenagers discovering the arts and artists that spoke to them.

Geddy Lee, lead singer and bassist for Rush, was born and raised in North Toronto by a working single mother. Massey Hall was not on her radar, so the youngster was left to discover the venue on his own. "For the kids of that generation of immigrants you were left on your own to discover the arts in your own way," he says.

Long before Rush took to the stage, Lee was a patron of this palace of the arts. The first show he attended there was on June 5, 1968. The band was Cream. This was one of the first rock shows presented at the venue and a harbinger of what was to come in the 1970s. It was a spectacular show and stands out as one of his fondest memories of Massey Hall. "I remember the day I went down to buy tickets. Strangely, none of my buddies wanted to go or they could not afford a ticket, so I went down to the box office by myself. The show was the same day Robert Kennedy was shot! I remember taking a short cut through Eaton's and Simpsons and in the section where they had instruments and television sets, all of the TVs were tuned to that horrible event."

Good music is a remedy for bad news. That's what Cream offered the teenaged Lee. He recalls this concert and its impact on him as a budding musician:

> In those days, when your heroes came on stage, they didn't even walk, they kind of floated onto the stage. I was just staring, especially at Jack Bruce because he was one of my first bass playing heroes and I couldn't get my eyes off his whole routine, how he sang and played the bass, and I remember there were only two microphones on the stage and they were going through the PA system of Massey Hall without having their own PA system! You've got this distorted voice of Jack Bruce and Eric Clapton while they were just rocking the joint.[10]

A crowd gathers outside Massey Hall before the 1965 centennial celebrations for the Salvation Army (which was founded by William Booth in 1865).

Jazz and Massey Hall are like-minded cousins. The spontaneity and improvisation of this musical style lends itself to the hall due to its intimacy and its superior acoustics. Similarly, some of the greatest modern blues artists, their music emanating deep from the soul, have also graced Massey's stage since the 1960s. Trumpeter and vocalist Louis Armstrong, an influential jazz pioneer, played Massey Hall several times in this decade. So did American swing balladeer Erroll Garner (March 5, 1962) and popular jazz pianist and band leader Stan Kenton (May 23, 1962). The queen of jazz, Ella Fitzgerald, was also a regular during the 1960s; she played for the first time in 1958 with Oscar Peterson, sharing the bill again in 1966 and 1976. Stan Getz and Duke Ellington made return engagements. Other jazz greats that took to Massey Hall's stage in the 1960s include bebop innovator Thelonious Monk (April 26, 1964); cool jazz pioneers Dave Brubeck (November 19, 1964) and Lionel Hampton (November 4, 1967), and the king of swing, Benny Goodman (April 27, 1968).

In 1965, Elmer Iseler made his debut as the Toronto Mendelssohn Choir's sixth conductor with four hundred performers in the Mendelssohn Choir Festival of Choral Music. The choir continued to perform regularly at Massey Hall until 1982, when it moved, along with the Toronto Symphony Orchestra, to the newly opened Roy Thomson Hall.[11]

Anyone who has ever met Richard Flohil, the affable and passionate music man, knows that time stops when he starts recounting one of his tales. Evidence of his eclectic career in music is on display in his Toronto apartment: a framed photo from Buddy Guy hangs on one wall; a photo with a young Serena Ryder is housed proudly in another frame; and hundreds of LPs, most notably blues and jazz selections from the likes of Sleepy John Estes, Son House, Muddy Waters, Sonny Terry, and Brownie McGhie, fill a cabinet on the floor opposite the couch.

Flohil arrived in Canada from England in 1957 and quickly fell into the local music business, first writing for the now defunct *RPM Magazine* and then promoting and doing publicity for live shows. In 1965, with a reputation Flohil says he had

IN PERSON
THE CREAM
MASSEY HALL
Wed., June 5th, 8:30 P.M.
Tix: 4.50—3.50—3.00
On Sale Massey Hall Box Office
and A & A Record Bar.

Cream, the psychedelic British trio of Eric Clapton, Ginger Baker, and Jack Bruce, was one of the first rock acts to play Massey Hall, performing on June 5, 1968.

Ella Fitzgerald and Oscar Peterson both played Massey Hall frequently over the years, including sharing the bill in 1958, 1966, and 1976.

"ill-earned" as a blues maven, he was asked to host a blues workshop at the Mariposa Folk Festival. "I had no idea what a folk festival was," he recalls. "I enjoyed the festival so much. It was very much an Isaac Newton moment. All I was into at that time was early American jazz and blues, and suddenly I'm discovering Buffy Sainte-Marie,

Leonard Cohen, Gordon Lightfoot, and Ian & Sylvia … it was like being hit on the head. It changed my life!"

Despite this discovery of a new genre of music, back in Toronto, Flohil was still known as "that jazz and blues promoter." So it's no surprise to learn he was the promoter who first brought bluesman Buddy Guy, and later Miles Davis, the legendary trumpeter and jazz trailblazer, to Massey Hall. But it was on Valentine's Day 1969 when Flohil promoted his first big-time show at the venue. The artist: B.B. King.

"I went to the manager of Massey Hall at the time, a guy called Joe Cartan. Joe said fine, I didn't need a deposit, he just trusted me." It was the bluesman's second appearance in Canada. Two weeks before the Massey gig he had played the Grand Theatre in Kingston, Ontario. Flohil had gone to that show with Buddy Guy, who was in town and had a day off, and Adam Mitchell, the lead singer of the Paupers. Making arrangements through King's agent in Houston, Texas, Flohil settled on a price of two thousand dollars (USD) to pay King for the gig. "I called up blind, said I'd love to book B.B. King for two thousand dollars, and Johnson said sure!" Flohil recalls. Ticket prices were set at $2.50, $3.50, and $4.50.

"I don't think it sold out," he remembers, "but it did very, very well. I had the good fortune to have booked an artist that, between the time I booked him and the time the show happened, had his one and only crossover hit, 'The Thrill Is Gone.' B.B. came in that day early and did a bunch of interviews with the local press. He catnapped in between interviews for ten-minute intervals. I don't recall too much about the show, but what I know is that I made seven hundred dollars."

Coretta Scott King, wife of Martin Luther King, Jr., sings at Massey Hall on May 15, 1966.

The last time Flohil saw King at Massey Hall, he was backstage as the bluesman was standing in the wings ready to go on. "B.B. saw me, hugged me, and said, 'You must have lost money all those years ago when we did that first show!' I said, 'No, B, I actually made seven hundred dollars and

"I arrived in the Yorkville coffeehouse music scene when I was eighteen and never left. And Massey Hall was very important to me.... My first show was as a fan. I quickly went from a fan of the hall to promoting shows for the artists I managed there."

— Bernie Finkelstein, promoter and former president, True North Records

you set me on the road to ruin!' He just grinned and said, 'Happy to have helped' and walked onstage."

Local music promoter Gary Topp attended all the folk shows presented at Massey Hall during the 1960s, and he was in the audience for another seminal show of that decade. "I was … getting into jazz at that time and Stevie Wonder was being touted as the next Ray Charles. I remember seeing Stevie's bus with all of these paintings decorating it parked in front of the building. The place was only half full. I don't remember much about the rest of the bill. 'Fingertips' was Stevie's big hit! The emcee invited everyone to stay for the second show because it was even emptier, so I moved

The king of the blues, B.B. King, pictured backstage on Valentine's Day 1969.

from the balcony to the tenth row on the floor. One week later [Stevie Wonder] celebrated his thirteenth birthday on *The Ed Sullivan Show*. I was older than the star on stage. That was pretty amazing."

Robbie Lane, along with his band the Disciples, was also on that bill. Lane was born and raised in Toronto. In the 1960s and '70s, Lane's band played regularly at Yonge Street clubs such as Le Coq d'Or and the Friar's Tavern. The timing of this memorable opening slot was good since the band's single "Fannie Mae" was charting on local radio station CHUM-FM. "When the promoter asked us to open for Stevie, it was an incredible opportunity," Lane recalls. "The 'Toronto sound' at that time, which my band was a part of, was based on R&B and blues. Stevie was one of the legends of that world. We were playing at Le Coq d'Or two blocks away from Massey Hall, six nights a week plus a Saturday matinee. We couldn't bring all our equipment down the street that quickly. The Coq d'Or's owner understood the importance of the Massey Hall invite and let us adjust our set times

Stevie Wonder first stepped onto Massey Hall's stage as a teen phenomenon in 1964. Toronto's own Robbie Lane and the Disciples shared the bill.

"My first time at Massey Hall, I was quite young. There was an R&B show ... Ray Charles [played] and this organ musician by the name of Doc Bagby and a couple of other artists. I thought this was a really high-class event. Something about it was really beautiful and also dark."

— Robbie Robertson, musician and songwriter, The Hawks, The Band

## Bob Dylan and the Hawks, November 14, 1965

It was November 14, 1965, when Bob Dylan and the Hawks pulled into town for a gig at Massey Hall. Rarely in its existence, during a musical performance, had boos rained down from the upper reaches of the hall's gallery. The show had sold out, so why the negative reaction? The crowd watched as the man they had come to hear — the poet Bob Dylan — the singer-songwriter whose every word they hung on and who spoke for their generation — plugged in, turned up the amps, and to their horror began playing an electric guitar; his backing band (members of the Hawks, who would go on to form the Band two years later) followed his cue, playing songs such as "Tombstone Blues." For many fans — the dyed-in-the-wool folkies who worshipped Dylan for his acoustic side — this was blasphemy. Dylan shrugged it off. He was just following his muse.

Bob Dylan, with the Hawks, went electric on November 14, 1965; boos rained from the rafters.

By the time the tour arrived in Toronto, they had already faced a similar reaction in other cities. The audience was divided; so was the media. Some fans stayed, but many exited in disgust, disillusioned once Dylan picked up his electric during the second half of the show. The *Globe and Mail* headline the next day was "A Changed Bob Dylan Booed in Toronto."[12] *Toronto Star* critic Anthony Ferry called the Hawks "a third-rate Yonge Street rock 'n' roll band." Of Dylan, he summed up the electric performance as follows: "That great voice, a wonderfully clean poet's voice, is buried under the same Big Sound that draws all the Screamies to a Beatle orgy of pubescent kids at Maple Leaf Gardens." Meanwhile Ferry's *Star* colleague Robert Fulford found the acoustic half boring, while the electric set offered "great waves of sound roaring off the stage in marvellously subtle rhythms ... it's Dylan's own new thing. I love it," he raved.[13]

that night. We did a thirty-five-minute set at Massey and then rushed back up the street to play our nightly gig at the club. Because we had to leave, I didn't see Stevie perform, but I did meet him backstage; that was a thrill."

• • •

In 1965 before forming the Band, Canadian Robbie Robertson was on tour with Bob Dylan as part of his backing band, the Hawks. He played the infamous Massey Hall show and for him, a young musician still growing up with the Hawks, the dismissal by Torontonians was almost too much to take. To return home, with many friends and family in the audience, and get greeted with jeers and hissing instead of cheers and whistling, stung. He had even told Bob not to worry about the crowds booing at Massey Hall. "That's our hood," Robertson recalled in his 2016 memoir *Testimony*.[14] "We are going back there and the people love us in Toronto." Robertson expanded on this, remembering the excitement of this homecoming:

> What a way to return home playing the classiest concert hall in town. All the guys were jazzed about seeing old friends and showing off a little. I took Bob over to my mother's house for one of her specialty meals, but ended up eating both my portion and Bob's. For our first night at Massey Hall, friends and family came out in droves to witness their native sons play the big time. We had gangsters and thieves, hustlers, tailors, cooks, contortionists, carnies and gamblers, you name it. John Lee Hooker was in town.[15]

LIVE AT MASSEY HALL

## Gordon Lightfoot, *Sunday Concert*, 1969, United Artists

*Sunday Concert* was Lightfoot's last record for United Artists and his first ever live recording, captured at Massey Hall in March 1969. The album includes performances of five previously unreleased tracks. It is also the first time that later hits and fan favourites "Ribbon of Darkness" and "I'm Not Sayin'" were recorded together as a medley. In 2012, Lightfoot released *All Live*, featuring his best performances captured by Bob Doidge at Massey Hall from 1998 through 2001.

Simon & Garfunkel, one of the most popular folk duos of the day, played Massey Hall in 1967.

What Robertson forgot was that Toronto, at the time — especially Dylan followers — remembered him playing acoustic music earlier in the decade in the Yorkville folk scene:

> We go out and they boo us more than anywhere else we had played. It was shocking! What we didn't realize was that Toronto — besides Greenwich Village — was the biggest folk music centre in North America with the whole Yorkville scene. We didn't know that! We didn't have anything to do with Yorkville and the coffee houses; folks weren't sipping coffee where we were playing. We were shocked and it hurt our feelings! We felt like we were hurting Massey Hall. It was really painful. If we had played somewhere else, it might not have stung as much, but Massey Hall is the ultimate prestige.

In *Testimony*, Robertson expanded on this rejection and its lasting effects: "Toronto was my hometown, and I took it personally. The city felt small and insecure, like it would never be important enough. When we left town after those shows I really didn't know if I would be coming back."[16]

As the 1960s drew to a close, Massey Hall had survived yet another decade. More memorable names were added to the historic list of performers who have graced its stage. Nashville and country music was well represented. Similar to what we will see continue in the 1970s with many of the folk acts and singer-songwriters that played Yorkville getting big enough to fill Massey Hall, the same occurred in the 1960s for many country artists such as Johnny Cash, Bill Anderson, Kitty Wells, Charley Pride, and Hank Snow, who had previously played much smaller Toronto venues like the Edison Hotel, the Horseshoe Tavern, and the Mutual Street Arena.

Talk of the future of Massey Hall and its viability continued. As the new decade began, it was becoming clearer that more money needed to be invested in the aging building. And the TSO were growing increasingly unhappy with the acoustics, which they claimed were not suitable for classical music, and the lack of adequate storage facilities and dressing rooms. It was becoming more and more likely that at some point the hall's primary tenant would abandon it for greener pastures. These realities reinforced the lingering question that the leaders of the hall and promoters grappled with as the tastes and entertainment demands of Torontonians and Canadians changed: Was Massey Hall still relevant and viable? One of the first huge records of the 1970s would be *Bridge over Troubled Water* from the folk duo Simon & Garfunkel — a harbinger of Massey's immediate future, perhaps?

# CHAPTER 5

## Let There Be Rock: The 1970s

The 1970s opened with Simon & Garfunkel releasing *Bridge over Troubled Water*, their final record together, and closed after the invention of the CD in 1979. In Canadian politics, Prime Minister Pierre Elliott Trudeau invoked the War Measures Act to curb civil liberties following the October Crisis in Montreal. On the world stage, the Vietnam War raged on. In music news, the Beatles broke up; punk arrived. So did disco.

One of the earliest bands of the fledgling punk rock scene, the New York Dolls, played Massey Hall on June 15, 1974, with future rock icons Kiss opening. A

◂ A boisterous crowd at Crowbar's seminal concert held September 23, 1971.

couple of years later, "punk poet laureate" Patti Smith played the hall. Canadian New Wave pioneers Rough Trade rolled in on December 19, 1977, with a show called "Restless Underwear" that mixed theatre and music. Kevan Staples, co-founder of Rough Trade, along with Carole Pope, recalls this unforgettable art meets music extravaganza:

> The "Restless Underwear" show was a blast. Imagine selling out Massey Hall with a theatrical musical extravaganza without being a recording artist. Peter Goddard gave us an unfavourable review, but the audience seemed to enjoy it. [Drag artist] Divine was lovely and we were thrilled to have her do the show. Carole and I were huge fans and had seen her stage appearances in New York. We were lucky to have Fran Pillersdorf, who had done two of Bowie's tours, hook us up with both Divine and Ron Link who directed the show. It was trashy and silly. Also worth noting that the show also had Luci Martin, singer from Nile Rogers's band Chic, as one of the trashy girls. Carole and her sister Elaine wrote the show and many of our friends contributed to the wardrobe and sets. We had dreams of taking it to New York, which we did a year later, where we bombed miserably due to the audience wanting none of us and much more of Divine. It was a humbling experience but somehow still worth the pain. It would be over three years before we got to play Massey Hall again. It is such a wonderful place to perform.

The Bee Gees, pictured backstage at Massey Hall in 1974.

Disco was represented by the Bee Gees, the trio of Gibb brothers who became the central force of the disco movement of the mid- to late 1970s; they played a pair of shows on February 17 and 18, 1974.

Meanwhile, many Yorkville folk artists and performers of the sixties previously booked by local promoters "The Bernies"

(Bernie Finkelstein and Bernie Fiedler) had achieved enough success to move their act to the storied stage farther south. The 1970s at Massey kicked off with a New Year's Day show from the Byrds. In the first two months of the decade alone, Massey Hall hosted a seventy-fifth anniversary show from the Toronto Mendelssohn Choir, a homecoming of the Band, and appearances by Loretta Lynn and Duke Ellington. The year ended with a packed December that included performances by Miles Davis, Leonard Cohen, and James Taylor, in addition to the annual Christmas traditions — the TSO performing *The Messiah* and several St. Michael's Choir School concerts. Country music was also still a popular draw throughout this decade. Besides Lynn, the likes of other greats of the genre appeared, such as George Jones, Crystal Gayle, Merle Haggard, Conway Twitty, and Hank Snow.

Dolly Parton and Porter Wagoner were one of many Nashville country acts that played Massey Hall in the 1970s.

"My first solo concert at Massey Hall was in 1976 when I was twenty-two. It felt like an honour.... I walked onto the stage ... barefoot. I'd released two albums. At the conclusion of my concert several people from my record company rushed the stage with two Gold albums, based on the sales of those two albums. I was overwhelmed, humbled. But then, seemingly out of nowhere, my parents rushed the stage. Bam! That was it. The peak of my career. I will never forget that thrill."

— Dan Hill, singer-songwriter

The hall continued to offer a diverse range of artists, from Indian sitar virtuoso Ravi Shankar and Greek composer Yannis Markopoulos to Canada's "First Lady of the Guitar" Liona Boyd; from a long list of American singer-songwriters like Laura Nyro, Melanie, Bette Midler, and Janis Ian, to Russian-born German vocalist Ivan Rebroff, French singer Alexandre "Sacha" Distel, American-born Greek soprano Maria Callas, American soprano Beverly Sills, and Canadian contralto Maureen Forrester. The decade also witnessed the capturing of three of the best live records ever recorded at Massey Hall — what would become classic albums by Neil Young, Rush, and Crowbar.

Debates about the hall's future did not abate in the 1970s. Local politicians and Massey board members met with consultants and developers about a proposed new hall. As early as 1972, city officials announced they would provide the site for a new hall as part of a massive development proposal called Metro Centre to be located west of Union Station and south of King Street.[1] Talk of this so-called "New Massey Hall" raged on. All the while, the Grand Old Lady of Shuter Street kept its doors open and continued to showcase not only international stars, but rising domestic talent.

Massey Hall always supported homegrown talent. The TSO and Mendelssohn

Choir found a permanent home here in its early existence; it's the stage where musical geniuses like Glenn Gould and Oscar Peterson performed regularly. The venue has always valued its role as a place to provide opportunities for Canadian artists to shine. In the 1970s, this unofficial mandate was noticed in the programming, with dozens of Canadian musicians making their debuts on Shuter Street. The Band returned home on January 17, 1970. Closing out the first year of the decade was a show on December 7 by Leonard Cohen. Anne Murray was one of the first homegrown female stars to grace the hall's stage.

When people hear the word *snowbird* today, the first image that comes to mind is of retirees migrating south to avoid the snow and cold of a Canadian winter. But if you flash back to 1970, it was the title of one of the most popular songs on the planet. Written by Canadian Gene MacLellan, but made famous by fellow Canadian Anne Murray, the ballad reached number two on Canada's pop charts and number one on both the adult contemporary and country charts. On the strength of the song's success, Murray became the first solo female artist in Canadian history to receive an American Gold record. It changed her life and paved the way for her Massey Hall debut in 1971. For two days (April 16 and

"In February of 1978, in between playing a concert in the U.S. with Anne Murray and flying down to be the soloist with the San Salvador Symphony, I was thrilled to pieces to finally be performing on the very same stage in which Bob Dylan, Joan Baez, Gordon Lightfoot, Nana Mouskouri, and others had captivated me. I believe it sold out and we were all thrilled. I'd had the idea to ask for a semicircle of palm trees around me to add interest to the bare stage, and I recall my English parents trying to cram a few into their VW van after the show."

— Liona Boyd, Canada's "First Lady of the Guitar"

Anne Murray went from playing the Imperial Room at the Royal York Hotel to Massey Hall's stage in a short time. Her debut was April 16 and 17, 1971, playing four sold-out shows over two days.

17), Murray played two sold-out shows each night. Rock trio the Stampeders, who were also riding high on the success of their recent single, "Sweet City Woman," opened. Despite not knowing much about the hall's history — and those who had performed there before her — stage fright struck the young singer. That experience taught her a lesson she carried with her throughout her career.

> That was my first time in a concert hall. I had played the Imperial Room at the Royal York Hotel, but had not been in an actual concert hall. That was a thrill, but I was scared to death. I remember wearing leather hot pants and a silk blouse. There was so much press going on around me. Before the show, I got together with a friend of mine; we got drunk, and that helped me relax. Not embarrassing, slurring-my-words, falling-down drunk; just as loose as a goose. The show suffered no unfortunate consequences from the drinking, and I had sobered some by the second show that night, but the experience — that sense of not being in full control of my faculties — scared me so much that I never did it again.[2]

In the late 1960s and early 1970s, Canadian country-folk singer Stompin' Tom Connors made his mark in Toronto at the Horseshoe Tavern on Queen Street. In fact, he still holds the record for the most consecutive nights played at the legendary bar (twenty-five). In 1972, the Canadian country outlaw released *My Stompin' Grounds,*

Stompin' Tom Connors was a fixture at the Horseshoe Tavern in the late 1960s and early 1970s. On February 4, 1972, he made his Massey Hall debut to a near sell-out crowd.

which featured the hit song "Tillsonburg." The album went Gold within seven months, selling nearly twelve thousand copies in the town of Tillsonburg alone. Tom had only ever played at "the Shoe" in Toronto, but he had his sights set on headlining a bigger stage — Massey Hall. Many in the music industry thought he was crazy. No way, said Tom's critics, could this East Coast yodeller, who sang quirky songs, pack the country's premiere venue. Filling a five-hundred-capacity club was one thing, but Massey Hall? Forget it, thought many; not going to happen.

But as Tom had demonstrated throughout his career, he didn't care what the industry or others said. He was dogged in his desire to achieve this goal. "Even though it scared me to think about it, I was determined that one day I would get to play in no less a venue than the great Massey Hall," he writes in his memoir, *Stompin' Tom and The Connors Tone*. "Everybody figured I was committing suicide in whatever musical career I'd been able to sustain up until now, because if nobody came to the show, I'd wind up being a laughing stock."

February 4, 1972, was booked for Tom's inaugural Massey show and the marketing machine began. Tom didn't just want to play the iconic soft-seater, he wanted to sell it out. "I heard the place could seat just under three thousand people when packed, and on February 4, I was planning to see what kind of a dent I could put in that magical number."

Connors figured he already had a dedicated fan following at the Horseshoe that would pay to see him at Massey, so he just needed to spread the news a bit further. He hired publicist Richard Flohil, who, as mentioned earlier, promoted B.B. King's first show at Massey Hall, to get the word out. Ads were placed in various publications and Flohil secured interviews with several newspapers to promote the show. "We distributed pamphlets under windshield wipers, in parking lots, supermarkets, hotel lobbies, grocery stores," Tom recalled in his memoir. "Nobody, at least from our side, wanted to see this show flop, so everyone just worked like a bunch of beavers."

Bill Haley, of rock 'n' roll pioneers Bill Haley and the Comets, backstage at Massey with his famed Gibson Super 400, during the 1970s.

The hard work paid off. On February 4, the people came — 2,800 strong. And as the curtain lifted, the chorus of "Bud the Spud" filled the hall, the sold-out crowd singing along as Tom stomped his cowboy boots to the beat. Recalling this moment in his memoir, Connors writes, "[The hall] had never seen this kind of a crowd before, and neither did a lot of these people have previous cause to come here before. It was like some kind of a revolution had taken place. The little man got to dine at the big man's table, and even got to choose his own style of entertainment."[3]

As Tom's widow, Lena Connors, explains, her late husband knew that a lot of great artists had played the hall and he wanted to be one of them. "It was something for him to play Massey," she recalls. "He always had butterflies for those big shows. Tom started out playing bars, high school auditoriums, and legions, and then was vaulted into a bigger scene. But Tom was never one to be awestruck. He was a man with a plan. He met all his goals over the years and Massey Hall was another feather in his cap, to quote one of Tom's favourite sayings."

Comedy featured prominently and frequently at Massey Hall over the years, from the early variety shows to stand-up comedy. During its history, the hall has hosted a who's who of comedic geniuses, including George Carlin, Max Bygraves, Canadian impressionist André-Philippe Gagnon, Lily Tomlin, Billy Crystal, Rodney Dangerfield, Billy Connolly, Robin Williams, Ellen DeGeneres, Sandra Bernhard, Jerry Seinfeld, Margaret Cho, and Wanda Sykes. The Just for Laughs Festival stopped in for several years and brought in the likes of Jimmy Fallon and Martin Short, and for many years, Yuk Yuk's impresario Mark Breslin hosted an annual New Year's Eve gala comedy night at the hall. The 1970s were a heyday for stand-up comedy at Massey Hall. A *Toronto Star* caption and photo following Victor Borge's 1973 show proclaimed that he "broke up [the] Massey Hall audience with his particular brand of patter and piano playing." Borge, a Danish-American humourist and musician, had previously played the hall back in 1959.

Comedians have always found a home at Massey. American stand-up legend George Carlin is one of the many who graced its stage.

Comedy duo Cheech and Chong (Richard "Cheech" Marin and Tommy Chong) called it their favourite venue in the world: "We used to save it for the end of every tour, like a great dessert," Marin told the *Toronto Star* before the pair's *Light Up America & Canada* tour came to town in 2008. For his part, Chong recalled taping the laughter and applause from those Massey Hall days in the 1970s and using the recording on their best-selling comedy albums and in their movies. "The acoustics there are the best," he said.

Working in the media, especially in the arts, gives one access to a lot of live shows. Whatever the medium (print, radio, or TV), as a journalist you get a different perspective of Massey Hall. Before getting into radio, Canadian broadcast industry hall of famer John Donabie attended his first show at Massey Hall in 1965, sitting front-row for the seminal Bob Dylan with the Hawks concert where Dylan went electric and the crowd booed. After Donabie landed a job at local radio station CHUM, he became a Massey Hall regular. CHUM, as the major player in the local FM rock-radio market during the seventies, presented many of the concerts at the venue, and Donabie was often called upon to emcee. "Massey Hall has always been great for me, especially in the 1970s," he recalls. "I was there all the time … it was like I lived there."

Singer-songwriter Arlo Guthrie chills backstage before his show at Massey.

Over the years, he figures he emceed more than a hundred shows at Massey Hall. "You would get there early and talk to the manager or the artist," he explains. "It was a very short conversation. They would usually instruct you on what to say. It was always thrilling." When he was booked to introduce folk pioneer Arlo Guthrie on November 12, 1974, the singer-songwriter threw him a curveball.

When Donabie introduced himself as the emcee who would be introducing him, Guthrie replied, "Come again? Really?" He then sat down and asked, "How does the house look?" Donabie told him it was jammed. "Do you think they know who is appearing here tonight?" He then asked, "So, tell me why I need you to introduce me to the crowd? Do you see where I'm coming from? Do you have two good seats, John? Just go enjoy the show. I'll walk out and they'll recognize me!"

Publicist Jane Harbury also visited Massey Hall often back then, usually entering via the stage door:

> After a while, the security got to know me. I remember when the Beach Boys came in the 1970s and I really wanted to hear them, but could not afford a ticket. I went around the corner to McDonald's bought some fries, then went to the side stage door and told my friend at security that I was bringing some food for one of the band members. He let me in! I never met any of the Beach Boys. I just went straight to the balcony and watched the show.

• • •

One of the biggest blues and R&B shows to hit the Massey Hall stage in the decade occurred on February 23, 1970. It was billed as "Blue Monday," and Richard Flohil told me, "everything that could go wrong did." The idea was to book a range of blues artists. He booked Bobby "Blue" Bland, who had never played in Canada before and came in with a big band. Also on the bill was Buddy Guy and, because the musicians' union at that time required a Canadian band on each bill, a band called Whiskey Howl. Flohil had also booked Sam Maghett (Magic Sam), but he got sick and cancelled, so he got Otis Spann, Muddy Waters's pianist who had started a solo career. At the last minute, Otis also got sick, so he made arrangements to have Lonnie Johnson, a local bluesman, play the show.

This last-minute addition provided a moving moment. Lonnie had been in a bad car wreck recently; then, while in hospital recovering, he had a heart attack and was partially paralyzed, so he couldn't play guitar anymore. That night, he came on stage, sat on a tall stool,

On "Blue Monday" (February 23, 1970), local bluesman Lonnie Johnson sings a pair of songs while Buddy Guy accompanies.

> "In Toronto, we don't have many venues that have a historic nature to them. We are not a city that preserves much in terms of our old buildings; many have been lost over time. One thing gets knocked down and something new replaces it. Somehow Massey Hall has remained. It's special from that point of view alone. It's an institution in a city that doesn't have enough institutions."
>
> — Geddy Lee, lead singer, Rush

and sang two songs. Buddy Guy accompanied him, playing every Lonnie Johnson lick there was. "It was incredibly moving," Flohil recalls. "A lot of Bobby's musicians wandered on stage and stood outside the spotlight just to watch. When Lonnie left the stage there were tears rolling down his face. He got a standing ovation when he went on and a standing ovation when he left two songs later."

Flohil later presented a show with Miles Davis. The jazzman was staying at the Four Seasons Hotel on Jarvis Street. The band showed up on time, but Miles was forty-five minutes late. "I remember manager Joe Cartan saying 'What are we going to do? We will have to give people their money back.' I go on stage to apologize and do this speech in front of the packed house. There is not one seat left, even the seats behind the pillars in the top balcony were sold. As I walked off stage, Miles Davis walked in the door, handed me his coat, took a trumpet out of his case, and went on stage and started to play."

The idea that you couldn't make it in Canada unless you made it in the United States first really started in the late 1960s. Joni Mitchell and Neil Young both saw their dreams come to fruition in California, while Leonard Cohen found success in New York. Europeans were much more aware of American acts and lumped Canadian artists in with them. In the early 1970s, the music press in the U.K. weren't aware of the variety of unique songwriters and groups that were emerging in Canada. Massey Hall has helped support homegrown talent throughout its existence: from booking some of the first performances from giants like Gould and Peterson, to being the stage where artists such as the Tragically Hip, Jann Arden, and Barenaked Ladies found an annual home decades later. So it's fitting that the venue was chosen to showcase our musicians to the world early in the 1970s. In 1972, music journalist Ritchie Yorke and Arnold Gosewich (president of Capitol

## Crowbar, *Larger Than Life (and Live'r Than You've Ever Been)*, 1971, Daffodil Records

A billboard advertising the concert hung high above Yonge Street. T-shirts were made. The show, held on September 23, 1971, was billed as "An Evening of Love with Daffodil Records." The concert was later released as the double album *Larger Than Life (And Live'r Than You've Ever Been).*

Numerous guests appeared with the band that night, including members of Lighthouse, Dr. Music, and Everyday People. King Biscuit Boy also returned to perform with his former Crowbar bandmates. The recording and release of the album are significant as being the first time a Canadian band had recorded and released a "live in concert" album. It was also the first time that a live concert was broadcast simultaneously on CHUM. *Larger Than Life* went Gold seventeen days after its release, becoming the first live album by a Canadian artist to do so. Frank Davies, who was then president of Daffodil Records, says the concert enshrined the band into Canadian rock 'n' roll folklore.

(top) Country music singer-songwriter Gary Buck was one of the many performers who took part in the Maple Music Junket – an industry showcase for the European press that took place over two nights at Massey Hall in 1972.

(bottom) The Mercey Brothers, a seven-time JUNO-award winning Canadian country music group, performs at Massey Hall as part of the Maple Music Junket in 1972.

Records Canada at the time) invited about a hundred European record producers and reporters to Canada for an all-expenses-paid trip to experience this emerging scene. Dubbed the Maple Music Junket, the trip included visits to Montreal and to Toronto, where a pair of memorable back-to-back shows occurred at Massey Hall. These gigs changed things for Canadian musicians. Once again, the hall played a key role in advancing and promoting our culture and artists to the world.

American country crooner George Hamilton IV, a regular at the Horseshoe Tavern in the 1960s, emceed the first show on June 6. The Mercey Brothers opened, followed by Christopher Kearney, Murray McLauchlan, Fergus, Bruce Cockburn, Gary Buck, and Perth County Conspiracy.

"This event was about trying to get us in the position where a Valdy, or any one of these Canadian musicians, could be a musician who doesn't rely on being a cover band," says Bill King, whose first time playing Massey Hall was as part of the Junket lineup backing up singer-songwriter Chris Kearney. "They needed to do something to say *we have an industry of artists who are developing that will be performing artists*. This is what the Junket was about."

The second night saw Edward Bear open, followed by Fludd, April Wine, Mashmakhan,

Pepper Tree, and Lighthouse. Hamilton rockers Crowbar capped off the evening, and they knew they had to make a statement despite the fact that the visiting journalists were worn out from the whirlwind trip. As Crowbar's drummer, Sonnie Bernardi, reflected years later, "We really had to do something to catch these fellas and entertain them."

And what an entrance the band made. As six bagpipers played "Amazing Grace," the stage came alive with lights and smoke to reveal a huge cardboard cake. Before Crowbar even started to play, a topless woman emerged from the cake, followed by the band members. Larger-than-life lead singer Kelly Jay was the last to appear, opening bottles of champagne, sharing it with those in the front row and spraying others in the audience. A high-energy set followed and not a soul in the hall remained in their seats, everyone standing up, clapping, hooting, and hollering. Bernardi believes Crowbar's performance made a lasting impression and even helped the band get the slots and venues they did when they finally toured in Europe.

It wasn't just Crowbar that benefitted; the Junket served to leave a lasting impression that helped to distinguish Canadian music from that coming out of America. In archival interview footage, one reporter states, "I thought Canadian music is the same like American music, but now I know the difference."

Valdy, Canadian folksinger, songwriter, and member of the Order of Canada, first played Massey Hall in the 1970s. He went on to record a live album (*Family Gathering*) at the hall in 1974. "I've played halls that felt bigger than Massey Hall, yet they sat a third of the people.... Every attendee leaves an energy in the hall, albeit small, but still a presence, so the feeling one gets is of performance history. Venerable is the word that best describes the hall."

Bazil Donovan first stepped through the doors of Massey Hall years before he became the bassist for Blue Rodeo and went on to play the venue thirty-five times. He, like

"By the time 'Down by the Henry Moore' came out, I was doing well enough where I could play there twice in the same year. Weird thing for me is I don't remember playing it that much. I thought only been there a few times — but it turns out I played there nine times between 1974 and 1980."

— Murray McLauchlan, singer-songwriter

(top) Genesis played Massey Hall in 1973 as part of a "Cheap Thrills" promotion.

(bottom) Cheap Trick's frontman, Rick Nielsen, asks the Massey faithful for some adulation in 1978.

**CONCERT PRODUCTIONS INTERNATIONAL Presents**

**CHEAP THRILLS#7**

**"Genesis"**

"The most intricate Theatrics since the Pink Floyd Show"

IN CONCERT, MASSEY HALL

**NOV. 8, 8 p.m.**

**RESERVED SEATING: $3.00 ADVANCE $3.85 DOOR**

Tickets available at all **Ticketron** Outlets (A&A downtown, Bloor, Newtonbrook) and Music World Stores in Yorkdale, Fairview and Scarborough.

many young Torontonians, first found his way to the Massey Hall stage as a member of his high school band; he played bassoon. Some of the earliest shows Donovan went to were country shows, which he attended with his uncles in the 1960s. One show that stands out in his memory, though, is the night in 1968 that he saw Procol Harum and King Crimson. He was only thirteen. Donovan, a consummate music lover, went on to see as many shows at the venue as he could afford to. Another date that still resonates for Donovan is November 8, 1973:

> I was seventeen and it was advertised as a promotion called Cheap Thrills — three dollars to get in (the normal prices were $5.50 or $6.50 for the best seat in the house). The band: Genesis, with Peter Gabriel as the front man. Half of their gear didn't make it. Half of their lighting show was [still] in Quebec. They said they had cobbled together enough stuff to do the show, but they were going to have to come back in six months or so and give us the real show. It was probably the most incredible show I have ever seen in my life. Peter Gabriel worked the room; they had not made it yet and they were working hard to. Phil Collins was

> just the drummer. He came out and sang one song. The hall was half full; it was the middle of the week. My friend [had] bought me a ticket. I went to the show not knowing what to expect. The next day I went out and bought every Genesis album … and they became, at that time, my favourite band. They came back six months later. I liked them so much, they did two sold-out shows and I went to both. You hear people talk about life-changing experiences … at seventeen, it rocked my world.

Growing up, Donovan was also a big King Crimson fan, and especially loved Bill Bruford's drumming. He thought if he cut school, went down to Massey Hall in the afternoon wearing a rock T-shirt, he'd look like a roadie and could sneak in to the show. What he didn't know at the time was that they hired local guys. The plan worked. "The moment I walked around the corner, the head guy says, 'Great, you're here, grab the end of this cabinet and follow me.' All of a sudden, I was working as a roadie for free. I didn't care. We started pushing gear around and I went for burgers with the guys on the crew. No one questioned me at all. Eventually the band came for sound check and there I was standing on stage with Bill

(top) Meat Loaf brought his larger-than-life sound and persona to Massey Hall on April 21, 1978.

(bottom) The Metropolitan Opera's soprano star Leontyne Price performed four times at Massey Hall during the seventies.

Robert Nesta "Bob" Marley brought his Rasta mysticism and reggae rhythms to Massey Hall in 1975.

Bruford and the rest of the band. I was just blown away. I couldn't believe I was standing watching them practise."

From the hall's opening in 1894 to the TSO leaving in 1982 for Roy Thomson Hall, classical music was a constant inside the three red doors off Shuter Street. Starting in the 1930s until the Canadian Opera Company was established in the 1950s, opera also found a home at Massey. Italian tenor Luciano Pavarotti made his Toronto debut there in December of 1973. Despite a top ticket price of fifty dollars (a record for the hall at the time), the show sold out. John Kraglund summarized the power of the performance of this "jovial mountain of a man," in the *Globe and Mail* the following day: "At the end of Sunday's concert at Massey Hall, it sounded as if Italian tenor Luciano Pavarotti had been staging a riot instead of singing a recital. The thumping, shouting, waving ovation is not particularly rare at operatic performances, but few opera singers manage to arouse a similar response in the concert hall, particularly after a recital that has included little opera."

With the arrival of more and more Caribbean and African immigrants to Toronto, beginning in the 1950s, what was referred to at the time as "world music" found a home in various venues around the city, including Massey Hall. Throughout the 1960s, groups from many different ethnic communities presented concerts at the hall — from performances by the Estonian Male Choir to a Calypso Fiesta show; from a headlining show by Indian composer and master of the sitar Ravi Shankar to a night with Spanish classical guitar virtuoso

Andrés Segovia. In terms of world music in the city, August 13, 1967, was a seminal moment. The record-breaking day for the Toronto Island Ferries saw thirty-five thousand people make the journey across the harbour to attend the final day of the city's newest music festival: Caribana — modelled on Trinidad and Tobago's Carnival.[4] A nascent local reggae and ska scene, a sound and style unfamiliar to Torontonians, started to develop. In the 1970s, Jamaica was the epicentre of the reggae renaissance. Robert Nesta "Bob" Marley was the prophet and musical messiah. Marley, in his only appearance at Massey Hall (June 8, 1975), opened with "Trenchtown Rock." The reggae rhythms he and his new backing band, the Wailers (this was the first tour and record without Bunny Wailer and Peter Tosh, who had left to pursue solo careers), wove on the crowd that night was more than a musical experience, it was mystical. Like the line from the chorus in this opening song, the audience left "feeling no pain."

Thirty years later, Peter Goddard, who worked as the *Toronto Star* music critic in the 1970s and early eighties, recalled it as the only "transcendent" concert he ever witnessed. "Something happened that night I still can't completely explain," Goddard says. "For years, I thought it was just the frame of mind I was in at the moment — and no, my thinking was not enhanced herbally, though I was nearly alone in that regard — until I heard through the grapevine that Marley himself had talked later about the show (his first in Canada) being special.... He darned near glowed on stage. It was as if he'd been created out of nowhere to do that one concert."

Musician Bill King concurs:

> That memorable night, righteous vibes blanketed Massey Hall. There were kids as young as three ... and seniors in their eighties fanning away the humidity. The event was akin to a Sunday morning revival. Women dressed in their finest while the kids wore their Sunday best. Obviously, Marley's music was something way beyond the pop ditties that temporarily sparked the brain then flittered away. These were songs that connected — songs that had an eternal feel to them — songs with a soul, a message, and a language all their own.

This was the *Natty Dread* tour, in support of the new Bob Marley and Wailers album released in 1974 and later celebrated in *Rolling Stone*'s top five hundred albums of all time. The album was a mash-up of writers, from the I-Threes to the rhythm section joining in.

Marley set the tone for the grand occasion by making a surprise appearance in the aisles leading to the main stage. He paused, kissed and hugged, shook hands, and sported a broad contagious smile that imprinted itself on every one of the 2,500 faithful in the room. Ticket prices that night? $7.50!

From the downbeat, the band played with the precision of a well-drilled military ensemble. They "skanked, skaed," and "reggaed" to a relentless groove, with guitarist Al Anderson applying the precise number of blues-coloured fills. The sound system couldn't handle the bottom-weight of Aston Barrett's thunderous bass lines. It was a night mostly buried under a blown sound system and persistent distortion. The saving grace — Bob Marley and his charismatic stage presence and arresting dance moves.

Marley and band played their eventual hits: "Trenchtown Rock," "Slave Driver," "Concrete Jungle," "Rebel Music," "I Shot the Sheriff," "No Woman, No Cry," "Natty Dread," finishing with "Get Up, Stand Up." It was as if an earthquake had struck Massey Hall. The aftershocks continued until the last person was evacuated. Seats vibrated, and feet stomped. Everyone screamed for more. Then Marley struck one last time [with "Nice Time"].

Tears, tears, tears. Everywhere you looked there were broad smiles and tears. The song is one of Marley's earliest singles — one remembered by a nation of immigrants and held close to the heart. It was the best of humanity on display. Mothers and fathers, grandparents and children embraced and swayed to the easy reggae beat and sang along. The prodigal son had come home![5]

In its 127-year history, Massey Hall has witnessed its share of magical musical moments. Neil Young's performances, beginning in 1971 and playing his most recent show in 2014, were definitely some of the most thrilling. The songwriter recorded an

"Massey Hall has always been great for me, especially in the 1970s. I was there all the time ... it was like I lived there."

— John Donabie, radio broadcaster

> "Neil played seriously great songs that night with more emotion than I had ever heard in live music up to that point. The energy and music were so powerful that even now it still reverberates in my mind. I feel my life is better for having had the experience of being on that tour."
>
> — Bernie Finkelstein, founder of True North Records

album there (*Live at Massey Hall 1971*), filmed a movie there (*Neil Young Journeys*), and most recently, in 2017, was inducted into the Canadian Songwriters Hall of Fame on its stage.

January 19, 1971, marked the first of these appearances. For Young, who was born in Toronto, stepping onto the Massey stage that night felt like a bittersweet homecoming. His father, Scott, and other family members were in attendance. Young had previously played Yorkville coffee houses like the Riverboat in the late 1960s to half-empty rooms and lukewarm receptions. But after finding commercial success in Los Angeles with the short-lived Buffalo Springfield and later with Crosby, Stills, Nash & Young, the songwriter returned home as a successful solo act. The event drew so much interest the promoter added an early show to meet the demand. "By early in 1971, there seemed to be nothing that he couldn't do," recalled Scott Young in his memoir *Neil and Me*. "We didn't talk money or sales, or anything similar at Massey Hall, but certainly part of his persona at that time was the huge success of *After the Gold Rush* — with sales of more than a million albums by then — and his share of the huge success of CSNY's *Déjà Vu*. The only fragment of conversation we had in that line at all was when I said to him, in the midst of the backstage crowd, 'Different from the last time.' 'Sure is!' he said."

Jack Batten captured this seismic shift in his *Globe and Mail* review of the show the following day: "All of a sudden, without anyone (except a million kids) noticing, Neil Young of Winnipeg and Toronto has arrived as a major pop star, someone to reckon with on the rich, heady, crowd-drawing level of James Taylor. If you don't believe it, you should have been

Singer-songwriter Carole King backstage at Massey Hall in the 1970s.

at Massey Hall last night where he played two concerts for sell-out houses of mostly young people who were there not merely to listen, but to worship."

Neil's producer, David Briggs, recorded the Massey show. After listening to it, he thought the live recording should have come out right away, and he disagreed with Neil's decision to instead put out his album *Harvest*. "He thought it was not as good as the Massey Hall recording," recalled Young in his memoir *Waging Heavy Peace*. As Neil later acknowledged, "When I heard the show thirty-four years later while reviewing tapes for my archive performance series, I was a little shocked — I agreed with David. After listening, I felt his frustration. This was better than *Harvest*. It meant more. He was right. I had missed it."

When Young finally released the recording in 2007, with Batten's permission he included Batten's review of the show on the CD jacket.

Rob Bowman, Grammy award–winning professor of ethnomusicology and author, was one of those young people in the audience worshipping Neil that night. "My first Massey Hall show was seeing Neil Young's debut in 1971. I was fourteen … I picked a good one! He played a number of unreleased songs … like 'Heart of Gold' and 'Old Man.' When *Harvest* later came out, I was stunned these songs sounded exactly the same. I remember it like it was yesterday and could show you my exact seat. I adored Neil and he mesmerized me. The hall itself seemed very special to me."

Since that night, which is now documented as one of the most famous concerts ever captured on tape at the hall, Neil has returned to play this musical house of worship eight times. And in 2009, seventeen Canadian artists, including the Cowboy Junkies, Colin Linden, Carole Pope, and Steven Page, gathered to pay tribute to this concert as part of Toronto's annual arts festival Luminato in a show titled "The Canadian Songbook: A Tribute to Neil Young's Live at Massey Hall." The artists recreated Young's 1971 performance, each picking one of the songs in his original setlist to cover.

A Paul Simon concert at Massey Hall, the Toronto stop of his *Still Crazy After All These Years* tour in the fall of 1975, was also a memorable one for all who attended. Promoter Rob Bennett describes how an electrical problem during the show fried the soundboard and the whole system went down. "Paul … handled it so well. He just stopped. The band left the stage and he played solo acoustic with no sound system. The techs worked on it and got it going eventually. It was magnificent. I had never heard anyone play there with no amplification … It was so special."

Former MuchMusic VJ Christopher Ward was also at the show and recalls this special moment. "It was a beautiful set; it looked like the New York City skyline. He launched into his first song and the PA system died before he started singing. People started getting restless. Paul picked up his acoustic guitar, walked downstage, and played with no sound system 'Homeward Bound.' It was breathtaking, fantastic, and made the show … there are so few venues where you have that option. The sound is so good and the audience is so quiet, it sounded amazing, like you were in his living room."

While many similar special moments in the hall have left indelible marks on the hearts and minds of thousands, other poignant memories are more individual. Murray McLauchlan recounts a personal story that the audience was surely not aware of but that stands out in his mind as his most important Massey memory:

San Francisco rock 'n' rollers the Tubes played Massey in 1975.

> It was January 26, 1974. My father was frail and on the way out at that point. That show was the first time he had ever come to hear me sing. We had been somewhat estranged up to that point, but we'd mended our fences and he'd decided to come.

## Bruce Cockburn, *Circles in the Stream*, 1977, True North Records

Recorded live at Massey Hall in the spring of 1977, during Cockburn's final shows on his first cross-Canada tour with a full band, this album captures Cockburn at his finest in a room where he was meant to play. The songs resonate and his acoustically inclined compositions sound beautiful inside Massey's walls. *Circles in the Stream* opens with Cockburn and his band being piped onto the stage; a standing ovation follows. From here, sixteen songs are presented – some of Cockburn's most popular up to that point in his career like "All the Diamonds," and "One Day I Walk," along with some new compositions ("Homme Brûlant (Burning Man)" and "Free to Be"). As the critically acclaimed journalist and author Nicholas Jennings writes in the liner notes for the deluxe digitally remastered version, released in 2005, "One of the marks of a great live album is the ability of the artist to inject his material with new vitality, to the point where even well-known songs take on fresh meaning. Bruce Cockburn did exactly that with *Circles in the Stream*."

"That album is still around and still sounds really good," says Cockburn. "The hall itself is a big part of the album. We played two nights. The second night went really well and almost everything on the record is from that night. I was very nervous. I remember looking out from backstage right before we went on and seeing some guy in the audience carrying on in some frantic way. Bernie [Finkelstein] has pointed this out to me a few times. 'You know what you said?' I do remember. I said, 'There is somebody I can yell at!' I was just so tense ... I was looking at ways to let it out."

Both of my parents, who were in the front row that night, were more than a little surprised that there was this large hall and it was completely full of people there to see me. I had them picked up in a stretch limousine and brought down to the hall — it had a phone in a silver handle, a bucket of champagne on ice, the whole nine yards. That's when my Mom and Dad realized I was going to be all right.

Canadian band Symphonic Slam made its only appearance at Massey Hall in a sold-out show on December 22, 1976, largely due to massive marketing efforts.

While many bands who have performed at Massey Hall have been regulars throughout their careers, others, for various reasons, have only stepped on that stage once. Symphonic Slam is one those stories. The *Toronto Star* headline screamed: "Colossal Ego Fills Rock Concert." On December 22, 1976, this relatively unknown group sold out Massey Hall at a ticket price of $2.99. Ray Furlotte, tour production coordinator, reflects on what he recalls as the best day of his life up until that point: "I stood on the stage at Massey Hall and watched my favourite band thrill the sold-out crowd of 2,760 fans who came on a freezing cold winter's night, three days before Christmas, to see the Toronto premiere of Symphonic Slam."

The Massey Hall concert was only the second performance of the current reincarnation of the band. The first had been a dress rehearsal and free concert at Sheridan College five days earlier. Symphonic Slam had started as a four-piece band out of Southern California in 1974. But by the

"As a fan, I've seen countless concerts ... Gordon Lightfoot shows, Bruce Cockburn's first show after he graduated up from Yorkville. I always walk out inspired. It's just a memory-filled place and I've always loved the acoustics. It's perfection."

— Jane Harbury, publicist

> "The idea of playing Massey Hall was the unattainable dream of every young player."
>
> — Geddy Lee, lead singer, Rush

## Rush, *All the World's a Stage*, 1976, Anthem Records

Rush would go on to record many other live shows throughout its forty-plus year career, but to this day, many fans call this record their favourite live album from the Canadian rock band. "It's probably the most raw album we've ever made," says Geddy Lee. The two-record set presented the band's hour-and-a-half headlining show in its entirety, a show that featured material from its first four Mercury releases: *Rush*, *Fly by Night*, *Caress of Steel*, and *2112*. *All the World's a Stage* would be Rush's first U.S. Top 40 charting album and would go Gold (50,000 sales) and eventually Platinum (100,000 in sales). According to the liner notes, this album marks the end of the "first chapter of Rush," and would mark the start of a trend of releasing a live album after each four-studio album cycle.

time of the Massey Hall show two years later they were a trio based out of London, Ontario — Timo Laine (synthesizer guitars), Jan Uvena (drums), and David Stone (keyboards). The Slam only had forty-two minutes worth of music from its debut album and one new song that would be on the upcoming second album. "This made it difficult in what type of situations that the band could play under," Furlotte says. "We also had a ton of equipment, bigger than most established rock bands, so we were limited to where we could play."

The band didn't have enough material to headline a big concert, so how did they manage to pull off the Massey Hall gig? "That was a special one-off showcase," Furlotte explains. "Slam's manager, Terry Sheppard, convinced A&M Records to underwrite the concert. There wasn't any opening act, as it would cost A&M more, so we showed a thirty-minute promotional concert video of another A&M Records artist, the Tubes."

Despite a few technical difficulties, and not being able to employ the band's usual pyrotechnics system because of the hall's fire regulations, the concert received great reviews. "The Slam headlining Massey Hall for only its second performance generated a lot of conversation in the Toronto music industry," Furlotte recalls. "Some bands that had been slogging it out on the high school and bar circuits for years couldn't believe what we did."

AC/DC's lead singer, Bon Scott, performs in 1979 when the Australian hard-rock band opened up for UFO.

• • •

Rob Bennett has promoted nearly seven hundred shows at Massey Hall. Like many who grew up in Toronto, his first time stepping into the building was as a teenager when his Grade 7 class attended a TSO concert. Later, he played on the Massey Hall stage as a drummer in his high school band during one of the annual shows for Kiwanis

Festival winners. In 1975, Bennett started promoting shows professionally. In January 1977, J.J. Cale was in town, with Prairie Oyster opening. At 7:30, as the crowd was coming in, a limo driver pulled up to the stage door and asked to meet the promoter. This twenty-five-year-old kid comes to the door and says to Bennett, "The Rolling Stones are in town and really want to come and see the show and hang out with Cale."

"I didn't even have seats to put them in, but I agreed," the promoter recalls. Bennett gave instructions to the head of security to notify him when the Stones arrived, so he could bring them backstage. He figured if the audience saw who was there, it would cause a stir. It turned out only Mick Jagger, Ron Wood, and Peter Rudge (their tour manager at the time) showed up along with a bunch of groupies. Bennett goes on:

> Wood was so drunk he couldn't stand and Cale is playing on the darkest stage you had ever seen. When the show starts, the stage manager usually turns the light off in the crossover hallway backstage because if the door ever opens, it cascades light onto the stage. At about 8:55 p.m., as Cale was starting his second song, this door opens and this huge blast of light comes through; it's Ron Wood and he is looking out and he just falls forward. Mick Jagger grabs him. I thought there was

LIVE AT MASSEY HALL

## Neil Young, *Live at Massey Hall 1971*, 2007, Warner/Reprise

Long before Young opened his vast archives and released this live show from 1971, a bootleg of this classic recording was a favourite trade among "Rusties" – Young's equivalent of Jimmy Buffett's "Parrotheads." After a couple of listens, it's no wonder why. *Live at Massey Hall* is an intimate experience, with just Neil and his trusty acoustic guitar. Throughout, Young displays his deadpan humour, talking about "in'eresting times" and giving the audience a sneak peek of many new songs. As you listen to "Old Man," "See the Sky About to Rain," "Journey Through the Past," and "Love in Mind," you can imagine the experience of having a seat at Massey and being privy to these then brand-new songs.

going to be riot as they were totally visible to everyone. I run backstage. I'm furious security didn't come get me to let them in. I get them back into Cale's dressing room. Wood is being propped up against the wall with a woman on either shoulder. His body had gone limp. I get a beer for Peter and Mick. About fifty minutes went by. They said [they were] really big fans and really want to see the show, so I took them out on the alley side where they just leaned against the wall and watched the rest of the show, and not a soul said a word! I was worried there was going to be a riot with people trying to get backstage, but there was nothing. The audience was so stoned! [The Stones] had just arrived in town and were scouting out a place to do a live record. I recommended the El Mocambo. I never spoke to them again. I was on the road in Edmonton when the show at the El Mo was happening (advertised as an April Wine show).

One week later, I was in Vancouver when a picture of Mick and I appeared in *Rolling Stone*, from that night at Massey Hall. The caption read: "Mick Jagger and friend backstage at Massey Hall at J.J. Cale, apparently where the plans were made for the El Mo show."

Promoter Rob Bennett with Mick Jagger backstage in 1977 at a J.J. Cale show.

# CHAPTER 6

## The 1980s

During the 1980s, Massey Hall survived another recession and the Toronto Symphony Orchestra departed its long-time home for the newly constructed Roy Thomson Hall. Music in the early part of the decade saw Dance and New Wave come into fashion, but rock still ruled. Michael Jackson's *Thriller* — the best-selling record of all time — landed in 1982, selling twenty-five million copies in that decade alone. Madonna was the most successful female artist, and MTV arrived on televisions across the continent. MuchMusic — Canada's equivalent to the U.S. all-music TV station — followed three years later. Video culture helped propel up-and-coming artists to new heights, and genres such as New Wave benefitted greatly from the new platform.

At Massey Hall, the decade began with folk stalwarts Judy Collins, Bob Dylan (a four-night stint in April), and Gordon Lightfoot (a ten-night run).

◂ Concertgoers often arrive at Massey Hall early to soak in the magic.

## The Police, November 24, 1980

The Police arrived in Toronto at a time when the band had experienced a meteoric rise; they were one of the most popular groups across England, Europe, and North America. The band opened with a medley of "Voices Inside My Head/Don't Stand So Close to Me."[1]

Most of that first year was dominated by TSO performances as its fifty-nine-year-tenure was coming to a close. During the 1980 election, the New Democratic Party held a rally at Massey Hall, and one of the speakers was a young member of Parliament named Bob Rae, who would be elected premier of the province. The year even saw the return of a boxing bout, with Sugar Ray Leonard taking on Roberto Durán. The night after the fight, U.K. sensation the Police performed.

Local promoters Gary Cormier and Gary Topp (the Garys) put on the Police show that rolled into town in November of 1980. The pair had previously booked the band for its first North American appearance two years earlier at the Horseshoe Tavern, where only a half-dozen people showed up to see the virtually unknown group from England. Now the band was back and on top of the world promoting their third album, *Zenyatta Mondatta*, which had been released earlier that fall.

Looking back, Cormier says it was the most incredible show he has ever witnessed. "As soon as the band walked on stage, the sound from those PAs was like standing next to a 747 engine, combined with all the screaming coming from the girls," he says. "It was quite awesome!"

The Garys had booked the building just two weeks before the show. While the band

> "Massey Hall has been an important part of my life and my musical education. One of my favourite shows ever was Frankie Goes to Hollywood. They played the song 'Relax' three times during the show!"
>
> — Kevin Hearn, Barenaked Ladies

A newspaper ad shows a pair of diverse shows held at Massey Hall in 1982: Iron Maiden and, a few days later, the Pointer Sisters.

was big enough at the time to fill Maple Leaf Gardens, the arena was not available. Since the Garys had a prior relationship with the Police, they got the gig and booked them into Massey. Ticket prices were set at fifteen dollars (a lot at that time). What the pair did not realize when they booked the show was that the TSO was rehearsing the same day. What this meant was that they could not get into the building until 4:00 p.m. Usually load-in for an 8:00 p.m. concert starts at 8:00 a.m. It takes the morning to set up, a break for lunch, and then sound check at 4:00 p.m. The crew was usually done by 5:30 p.m., giving them time for dinner before the show started. Pat Taylor, who was in charge of the union at the time, reassured Cormier: "We will make it happen!"

Steve Stanley, former member of Canadian indie rock band the Lowest of the Low, worked part-time as a Massey Hall usher for many years and was there for that gig. "That was a crazy night! We are down in the room; everyone has their uniforms on and we start hearing 'Walking on the Moon.' We went upstairs to watch the Police sound check; instead, it was three roadies playing a note-for-note version of the band's song. That was so cool!"

"I remember it's 3:59 p.m. and I'm standing there with the Police's tour manager, Pat, and all the union guys," Cormier says. "The last guy picked up the chairs, music stands, and then we had to load in an entire PA system: each speaker weighed five hundred pounds. Everybody was running around and worked until it got done."

Bazil Donovan, bassist for Blue Rodeo, who has seen hundreds of shows at Massey Hall and played there dozens of times, remembers this show well. It was one of the best he's ever seen. At the time, he was in a band called the Sharks, who Cormier managed. "I just went down and walked in with my son, who was six at the time and a big fan," Donovan says. "They played and it was the most incredible performance. They were so good … at the peak of their career. Their third album … had just come out. To see a band that was way bigger than that room, in that room at that time, was just phenomenal."

• • •

On June 4, 1982, the gala final concert by the TSO at Massey Hall took place and included music from its very first performance there back on April 23, 1923. Conductor Andrew Davis shared the podium with guest conductors Erich Kunzel and Elmer Iseler. The Mendelssohn Choir sang the Hallelujah chorus from Handel's *Messiah*. Many patrons came dressed in the fashions of the 1920s. One of the highlights of the night was the performance of "A Farewell Tribute to the Grand Old Lady of Shuter Street" by composer Johnny Cowell (a member of the trumpet section), which had been commissioned by the symphony to commemorate the end of an era. In the program notes, Cowell wrote: "Some time ago the idea came to me that I would like to write a farewell tribute to the Grand Old Lady of Shuter Street before the Toronto Symphony Orchestra moved out of Massey Hall.… What I finally wrote was my own personal feelings about a place where I have spent a good deal of my life."

• • •

Seeing U2 at Massey Hall in the fall of 1984 on their *Unforgettable Fire* tour was one remarkable night for radio personality John Derringer. "Sometimes you just feel you are in the presence of something incredibly special," he recalls. "You just knew you were witnessing, without question, the last time you would see them play in a venue of that size. I don't pretend to be a great predictor of musical trends, but you knew that these guys were going to be huge … I was in the presence of something very powerful that night."

• • •

Music for the entire family by Canadian acts is another genre that found a home at Massey Hall in the 1980s: from Raffi to Fred Penner to Mr. Dressup. But when it comes to children's entertainers in Canada, no one compares to Sharon, Lois & Bram (Sharon Hampson, Lois Lilienstein, and Bram Morrison). Generations of kids sang along to their records and danced to their music in their living rooms. Later, many of these same children attended shows at Massey Hall with their kids or grandkids. "Talk all you want about Springsteen bridging the generation gap. He isn't in Sharon, Lois & Bram's league," wrote Peter Goddard in the *Toronto Star* back in 1985. "The Sharon, Lois & Bram shindig at Massey Hall Saturday afternoon first appeared on most calendars under 'kids' stuff,' or 'things for children to do.' But that's only half the truth. Listen, this was a hot ticket, like Dylan's first time at Massey. Hot."[2]

At Sharon Hampson's home in North Toronto, a Massey Hall print with the trio's name on the marquee hangs just inside the front door — a daily reminder of the group's place in the hall's history. They performed at Massey Hall forty-seven times, starting in the 1980s, and would do two types of shows — one with a band and one with the

On June 4, 1982, crowds filed into Massey Hall to hear the TSO's final farewell gala concert. After sixty years as the hall's primary tenant, the TSO moved to the newly opened Roy Thomson Hall.

"As awesome as it is to sit in those seats, it's a very special experience to get up on that stage. You get to see the place from the other side."

— John Derringer, long-time radio host, *Derringer in the Morning*, Q107

On June 19, 1982, Rodney Dangerfield brought his comedic act to Massey; a young Canadian comic named Jim Carrey opened.

Toronto Symphony Orchestra. "We always loved playing Massey Hall," says Hampson. "I remember when we got the call to play there for the first time, I started to jump up and down; I was so excited. We had made it!"

"It feels like you are part of some serious history," adds Morrison. "Massey Hall is stacked so high.... It's like a wall of people because of the configuration. As a performer you feel that much closer to them. It's energizing to be that close to your audience and feel that strong a connection."

• • •

Early in her career, Jane Siberry played a trio of headline shows at Massey Hall (1985, 1988, and 1990). For musician Bill King, that first show was a very emotional experience. When the *Globe and Mail* asked him to name a few epic concerts that had moved him over the years, one he chose was Siberry's debut. "I can't explain why," he recalled, "but I wasn't alone in that room. I looked across the aisles and others were also in tears. It was magnificent. It was the voices, the ethereal sounds and high emotion."

"When I moved to Toronto in 1986, one of the first places I sought out was Massey Hall. I'd heard so much about the place — its history, who played there, its importance to Canadian culture — that I just had to see it for myself.... I've been lucky enough to work at Massey Hall many times since ... I'm hoping that when it reopens, I'll get to stand there again."

— Alan Cross, radio broadcaster and writer

Siberry told King that that first gig at Massey Hall (October 25, 1985) was a big step for her in many ways. "As I started to find my footing as a musician and even in the beginning, I would find people, when they tuned in to the emotional part of it — that's what people seemed to really like," she explained. "I started noticing that and Massey Hall was another leap for me because it was the first time I could actually hear myself when playing with a band. I could get super quiet and hear it come back like a crystal from the back, and [I] thought, *this is what music is supposed to be*, not struggling to play with a band and get through the songs."[3]

• • •

Many Massey Hall staff members, past and present, have been a part of one big happy family. Just like the patrons, most share a love of the venue. From the part-time ushers (many drawn from the arts community over the years) to the full-time employees, there is a bond that links anyone who has ever drawn a paycheque from the corporation. This familial feeling is what struck promoter Riley O'Connor from the first time he entered through its doors. "I walked in through the stage door and I was greeted by the security guy, who asked me who I was and what I did," O'Connor recalls. "The

(top) Children's entertainers Sharon, Lois & Bram played Massey Hall frequently over a twenty-year period beginning in the 1980s.

(bottom) Jane Siberry relaxes backstage after a performance at Massey Hall on October 25, 1985.

(top) Joan Armatrading performed at Massey in 1978, 1982, and again in 1985.

(bottom) In 1985, popular British reggae band UB40 played back-to-back nights, March 11 and 12.

next time I went back he remembered my name. There was this automatic sense you were making a connection and immediately you became part of what I call the Massey Hall family." Most employees loved the hall and had a history with the venue before getting hired. Nancy Beaton is just one example. Long before Beaton became a Massey Hall employee, she attended a concert there with her mom, and the event remains etched in her memory, especially the encore. She was about fourteen years old, and the artist was Nana Mouskouri, one of her mom's favourite artists. Mother and daughter sat in the side gallery. "Nana came out to do an encore, and she just stood at the edge of the stage and sang 'Ave Maria' a cappella, without a mic," Beaton recalls. "That was the first time I had ever heard anyone do that, and I'll never forget the sound up in the gallery, because it was like, *How can this be happening? How can we still hear her up here?* There were people standing and starting to leave and they would stop midway to the exits because the floor was creaking under their feet. I thought, *Wow — this place is amazing!*"

Beaton was born at St. Michael's Hospital, right across the street from Massey Hall. Perhaps it was her destiny to end up working there one day. But Beaton never imagined when she took the part-time usher gig during university that her tenure at the hall would last more than thirty years. Johnny Cash once called her "ma'am." And, in what she describes as one of the more awkward moments during her Massey Hall career, she had to introduce Gordon Lightfoot to Robin Williams. And each time she saw Stéphane Grappelli play the violin like an angel on that historic stage, she was transported to Paris circa 1930. The memories come back in waves. This is her Massey Hall story.

Flash back to 1987. That's when Beaton joined the staff at Massey Hall as a part-time usher. "I don't know why I ended up there," she says. "I always felt there was some sort of magical draw between Massey and me." When Andrew Lloyd Webber's Broadway musical *Cats* came to the hall in 1989, returning to the city for a second run after a stint in Montreal and a Western Canada tour (following its original two-year run at Toronto's Elgin Theatre), that's when everything changed, she says. "Up until that point I would tell people I worked at Massey Hall and they would say 'Is that place still open?' It was falling off the radar. Then *Cats* came. They renovated and put in air conditioning and that really helped. I don't know what would have happened if that didn't occur. Before the air conditioning, we couldn't have any shows in the summer. Maybe, we would have a few graduations in June, but we had to open fire exit doors to let the hot air out."

Nana Mouskouri has played Massey Hall more than any other woman in the venue's history, including a six-night run in 1986.

With the arrival of *Cats*, Beaton had a variety of jobs, working in the box office as well as in the front of the house. It wasn't long before she was offered a full-time position in administration. During the early 1990s, when the recession hit, the corporation was forced to downsize, and Beaton was one of the few who was kept on. "That was traumatic," she recalls. "All the full-time people were gone except the stage electrician, the building operator, and me. It was all part-timers. Suddenly, I was an event coordinator."

"At Massey, it wasn't about the party. If I wanted a party I would go to another venue. I went there for church ... for devotion."

— George Stroumboulopoulos, radio host

A real cast of characters has worked as ushers at Massey Hall over the years. Beaton recalls uniforms that consisted of red polyester jackets, blue skirts, and bow ties. When Michael Cohl's Concert

(top) A Massey Hall usher's jacket, from the 1980s.

(bottom) In 1989, after air conditioning was installed, the musical *Cats* took over Massey Hall for a nine-month run.

Productions International (CPI) leased the building for five years in the mid- to late 1980s, CPI co-presented shows along with Labatt Breweries, which poured more than $330,000 into the aging facility. Under the moniker Blue Live Entertainment, formed with Hamilton concert producer Jim Skarratt, they promoted more than a hundred shows a year at the hall. Consequently, the ushers had different uniforms for the CPI shows, which included a little white scarf with a Labatt Blue logo on it. Today, the skirts are gone and everyone wears pants.

As the 1980s made way for the nineties, Massey Hall weathered yet another economic downturn, eventually reclaiming its niche as the preferred place in the city for people to congregate. Somehow, Hart Massey's gift to Toronto had survived yet another decade. And within a few years, the cherished cultural epicentre would celebrate its centennial.

"Strange Animal" Lawrence Gowan performed his first solo show at Massey Hall in 1987.

> "The ushers really love Massey Hall, but also the bartenders, the ticket sellers, all the staff ... it's a real family.... There is something about working a show, or any kind of event. You are there all day setting up, anticipating everything that will go right, what could go wrong. You open the doors and everyone comes in and are having a good time. It's very gratifying."
>
> — Nancy Beaton, long-time Massey Hall employee

AMX FROM
BACK-HOUSE
DMX FROM
BACK-HOUSE
AMX FROM
BOOTH
PUSH
AMX FROM
CHOIR LOFT

# CHAPTER 7

## Canadians Take Centre Stage: The 1990s

Toronto in the 1990s witnessed a thriving music scene in the clubs scattered throughout the downtown core; from the Horseshoe Tavern on Queen Street and the El Mocambo on Spadina Avenue to Lee's Palace on Bloor Street and the Danforth Music Hall to the east, indie rock ruled. Canadian bands such as Barenaked Ladies, the Watchmen, Skydiggers, the Lowest of the Low, Our Lady Peace, and Sloan found DIY success initially and gained large, loyal audiences during the decade. Many of these bands progressed from the club circuit and eventually saw their names on Massey's marquee. The decade was also one of the most explosive and profitable for Canadian women artists on the world stage. Pop stars like Céline Dion (May 25–26, 1993), Shania Twain, Alanis Morissette, Sarah McLachlan (November 25–26, 1993), and k.d. lang (June 23–24, 1992) burst onto the scene. As noted, many of them headlined shows at Massey Hall in the 1990s.

◂ Sound at Massey Hall has always been more of an art than a science, but both are needed to create the aural experience.

Sarah McLachlan shines in her Massey Hall debut in 1993.

Another Canadian band that played Massey Hall in the 1990s was Vancouver's Grapes of Wrath (October 10, 1991). Kevin Kane, guitarist and singer in the band, remembers being super stressed that day because it was such a big deal to play there. For the occasion, promoter Elliott Lefko presented each of them with a pair of monogrammed socks.

> A lot of it is a blur, but I do remember one highlight. Our shows at that time could get pretty out of hand, with kids constantly clambering onto the stage while security did their best to catch them before they got to one of the musicians — it was kind of a game for them. At one point, a young man leapt from the balcony to the stage (about a 6-metre drop), landing right in front of me with a resonant 'boom.' We looked at each other, shook hands, and he did a graceful backward dive off the stage and into the audience just as a security person was about to grab him: classy! It seems that any time I meet anyone who was at that show they bring that up.

The decade was one of continued diversity in the hall's programming and saw the return to the storied stage of many past performers. Then there was the celebration

> "It's a special feeling the first time you walk in those stage doors."
>
> — Gord Sinclair, bassist, The Tragically Hip

of the hall's centennial, which included the opening of a bar onsite and the availability of alcohol for the first time in the venue's history. The basement bar was aptly named Centuries. This watering hole became the place for many patrons to congregate before shows. The walls lining the entrance to the bar were decorated with displays of newspaper clippings and ads highlighting past shows, speeches, and artist appearances by decade, covering the first hundred years of the hall's existence. This mini museum wall was always a must-stop spot for any artist playing the venue for the first time.

Canadians took centre stage (literally) at the venue throughout the decade: from Stompin' Tom Connors (October 24–25, 1990; October 29, 1998; September 18, 1999) to the Tragically Hip, Barenaked Ladies, and Blue Rodeo to Amanda Marshall, Jane Siberry, Cowboy Junkies, and Great Big Sea. Increasing in popularity by leaps and bounds at the time, hip-hop was represented by a performance by rapper LL Cool J in 1991. Other musical highlights from the 1990s include Ronnie Hawkins's sixtieth birthday bash (January 12, 1995), back-to-back nights with the legendary Aretha Franklin (April 7–8, 1993), a solo Bruce Springsteen show (January 8, 1996), a couple of dates by

The program for the street festival held to honour Massey's centennial on June 12, 1994.

(top) To celebrate the hall's one hundredth anniversary, Centuries bar was opened in 1994.

(bottom) During the late 1990s, Stompin' Tom Connors finished every Canadian tour at Massey Hall by auctioning off his stompin' board, which protected the stage floor from his pounding heel, for charity. Connors poses here on September 18, 1999, with auction winner Hugh Gillis (left), whose $5,000 bid went to the Daily Bread Food Bank.

Johnny Cash, and solo performances from two of classic rock's biggest guitar gods — the Who's Pete Townshend (July 10, 1993) and the Rolling Stones' Keith Richards (February 6, 1993). There was even a show at the end of the decade from Iron Maiden; yes, you read that right: one of the world's biggest heavy-metal bands, known to sell-out stadiums around the world, played Massey Hall on July 20, 1999.

Outside of music, programming also included a talk by the fourteenth Dalai Lama, Tibetan spiritual leader and recipient of the Nobel Peace Prize, who brought his message of "compassion for all sentient beings" in 1990. And comedy continued to be a big draw, with improv shows by the Royal Canadian Air Farce and stand-up performances from Andrew Dice Clay, Billy Connolly, Jeff Foxworthy, Ellen DeGeneres, and Victor Borge, a Massey Hall regular over the years.

Nancy Beaton, events manager at Massey Hall, says her most memorable show occurred in this decade: Sinéad O'Connor in May of 1990, when the Irish singer-songwriter was touring in support of her second album, *I Do Not Want What I Haven't Got,* which won a Grammy that year for Best Alternative Music Album and a JUNO for International Album of the Year.

> I was near the back staircase and heard screaming. I thought something terrible had happened. I remember running up the back stairs and into the auditorium afraid of what I would see. It was just people cheering for her. It was like Beatlemania! Nobody competes with Sinéad for intensity … she is magical. That was the first time I heard how loud it could be in there and how powerful the audience can be.

It was onstage at Massey Hall that the Tragically Hip first drew international attention. Though they were only scheduled to play two songs at the 1988 Toronto Music Awards, MCA's Bruce Dickinson flew up from New York City on an invitation from the band's manager, Jake Gold, to see those six glorious minutes of the Hip. "During the first song, Gord [Downie] drops the microphone, it splits apart and comes unplugged," Dickinson recalls. "The band does not miss a note. I saw a group that was not going to be rattled. They were already pros. I turned to Jake and said, 'I want to sign your band.'" British journalist Chris Roberts of *Melody Maker* magazine, in town to see Mary Margaret O'Hara, pronounced them "the discovery of the night."

The hype was justified: only four years later, the *Globe and Mail*'s Elizabeth

Irish singer-songwriter Sinéad O'Connor was a worldwide star when she played to a sold-out Massey Hall for the first time in 1990 and again in 1997.

> "It takes a long time to play Massey Hall properly. If you just play like you are in a bar, it is really too loud and the dynamics are flat. It is so ambient and sonically perfect. You just have to play quietly and play loud and learn how to work the dynamics. That took us ten years."
>
> — Jim Cuddy, Blue Rodeo

Renzetti witnessed one of their two sold-out nights at Massey Hall and had this to say: "Downie said little to the crowd, but he didn't have to — every eye in the house was trained on him. Every rock 'n' roll band should have such a lead singer," she added. "People who love the Tragically Hip cannot understand why anyone with their faculties intact would not."

The quintessential Canadian band played Massey Hall a total of nine times, and each was a seminal moment. The weight of the place was never lost on these Kingston rockers. "Massey Hall is the pinnacle," explains bassist Gord Sinclair. "It's where you aspire to play. There is just something so special about its aura and the feeling of playing on that stage. It's a place of communion. It's a congregation between doctors, lawyers, blue-collar workers, and everyone in between. Everyone is there for the same reason: to share an experience. It was a venue circled on our calendar as the high-water mark from the moment the Hip started out. I still get goose bumps just thinking about all of our performances there."

• • •

Ed Robertson of Barenaked Ladies grew up in Scarborough. Unlike bandmate Kevin Hearn, he never played at or visited Massey

> "It meant a lot to return there as a grown up on my own terms, with my own project, in that space. By the time I was older, I could appreciate more the history of the place and how many seminal shows had happened there: from the famous jazz concert to Neil Young."
>
> — Kevin Hearn, Barenaked Ladies

Hall with his school. The first time he went there was to see the Kim Mitchell Band in 1986; however, he was aware of Massey's legacy long before. "I was such a Rush nerd growing up and knew *All the World's a Stage* had been recorded there," says Robertson. "I think my parents saw Lightfoot there once in the late seventies, as well."

Flash forward to 1992. That's the year Robertson and his Barenaked Ladies (BNL) bandmates released their studio debut *Gordon*, an album that has now sold more than a million copies in Canada alone. On the success of this release, the band was booked for four sold-out nights at Massey Hall in April 1993. The first of these shows was broadcast live on local alternative radio station CFNY — not bad for a band that used to show up at that radio station's lobby and play for free. Since then, the band has played the hall regularly over the past few decades. For the BNL frontman, that first string of shows is still so special, mostly because his childhood heroes sent them a bottle of bubbly. "That's what I was most excited about," recalls Robertson, who does not drink but walked around with that bottle for twelve hours, "the fact Rush knew we existed!"

BNL went on to play the venue more than a dozen more times after that four-night stand, but besides all of the matinee shows they did for kids following their children's record (*Snacktime!*, 2008) and Christmas shows they performed at Massey Hall, one other night that stands out for the band is November 13, 2015. That's the evening when Dee Snyder (Twisted Sister's frontman), who was in town performing in a play, joined the band onstage for the encore to sing his 1980s hit song "We're Not Gonna Take It." "Alan Doyle opened that show and he stood watching this moment from the side of the stage," Robertson recalls.

(left) Beginning in the 1990s, following the success of their studio debut *Gordon*, Barenaked Ladies were Massey regulars.

(right) The Rolling Stones's guitarist, Keith Richards, played a memorable solo show at Massey Hall in 1993.

"Alan says it's one of the top five musical moments of his life and he wasn't even involved! His guitar player had to hold him by his belt to prevent him from walking on stage."

Keith Richards rolled into Massey Hall on February 6, 1993, as part of the X-Pensive Winos's fourteen-city tour in support of the Rolling Stones' guitar-slinger's second solo album, *Main Offender*. In an interview with *Maclean's*, Richards spoke about his love for soft-seaters like Massey Hall. When the interviewer asked him where he felt most comfortable, at the SkyDome or the Shuter Street shrine, Richards replied, "Massey Hall anytime. Give me four walls and a ceiling so I hear those drums coming off the back wall."

• • •

Lawrence Gowan was born in Glasgow, Scotland, but grew up in Scarborough,

Ontario. In recent years he's been touring the world as lead singer for 1970s classic rockers Styx. The first time he played Massey Hall was for two sold-out nights on his *Great Dirty World* tour in May 1987. "It is a very pivotal place for me in a lot of ways," Gowan says of the venue. And, while he has many memories of playing on that storied stage, being asked to be a part of Ronnie Hawkins's sixtieth birthday party in 1995 was definitely the highlight. (Back in the early 1980s, Gowan had been part of Hawkins's band.) On that night, he sang three songs — one of his own ("When There's Time for Love") and a pair of Little Richard classics.

"My piano was facing Jerry Lee Lewis to my left, and Jeff Healey, Carl Perkins, and



## "Let It Rock!" (Ronnie Hawkins's sixtieth birthday celebration), January 12, 1995

"There's gotta be a thousand years of knowledge at least right here on this stage!" said the Hawk (centre) a few minutes after completing the song that opened the ninety-minute program "Let It Rock!," an all-star tribute to celebrate his sixtieth birthday.[1]

A nineteen-piece rock 'n' roll dream band that featured Carl Perkins (right), Jerry Lee Lewis (left), members of the Band (original Hawks Levon Helm, Rick Danko, and Garth Hudson), Jeff Healey, and Lawrence Gowan backed Hawkins. This show was one of the last times both Danko and Perkins performed live.

Levon Helm were behind me.… It had the feeling of it being rock 'n' roll heaven. I was a classically trained guy, but I loved that the place was a spot where you could legitimize rock music: the TSO and Rush belonged on that stage in equal measure," said Gowan.

• • •

Tom Wilson (of Junkhouse, Lee Harvey Osmond, and Blackie and the Rodeo Kings) first appeared on Massey's stage when he opened as a solo act for Jeff Beck. Later, as a headliner, he performed with Blackie and the Rodeo Kings. He loved hanging out in the old dressing rooms and would always get to his gigs early enough to soak in the history. "People say Mojo, but I hate that term," Wilson says. "There was a little bit of the spirit of those who had sat there before me, like Charlie Parker, Lou Reed, Bob Dylan, and Lightfoot. What I loved, more than walking out on that stage that first night, was just sitting in my own room backstage."

One of Tom's favourite stories about the hall took place one January night in 1996 when Sony Music (his publisher and record label at the time) invited him to be Bruce Springsteen's guest and meet the Boss backstage. Apparently, the twenty-time Grammy winner had heard Tom's song "Jesus Sings the Blues" and really liked it. "He wanted to meet me because he liked my song," Tom recalls.

> I go down to Massey Hall and there are two backstage passes waiting for me, along with a pair of front-row [tickets] … sitting way too close, closer than I've ever sat for any show at Massey Hall (it's the kind of thing you want to crunch down in your seat and hide because the performer is looking at every part of you). I'm

"I would always go back into my dressing room at the end of the show with an incredible feeling of elation. My own musical spirit had linked arms with this history. It takes you back to another era and you think of all the music that happened there. It's lofty, but you think about those things in Massey Hall."

— Lawrence Gowan, musician

sitting there and Bruce Springsteen comes out, just him and an acoustic guitar. It was the *Ghost of Tom Joad* tour and he was wearing only a leather vest and no shirt. After the show, I went backstage. I was the last person to meet Springsteen. I go into the smallest dressing room on the eastern side of the building. The record company representative says, "Bruce, this is Tom Wilson; he wrote that song 'Jesus Sings the Blues.'" And then Bruce says to me, "Well, if Jesus sang, he certainly would sing the blues, wouldn't he?" That's a great Massey Hall memory for me!

• • •

"For me, as a teenager looking back, it was like a listening room: a comfortable, familiar surrounding that no matter what I was going to see, that room was going to capture something in the performance and in the audience and it was going to connect."

– Tom Wilson (Junkhouse, Blackie and the Rodeo Kings)

Best known as a VJ for MuchMusic, George Stroumboulopoulos later worked for CFNY and CBC. Today, he hosts *The Strombo Show* each Sunday night on CBC Radio. Sitting in his home studio in a pair of Massey Hall chairs (part of a limited number of 1948 seats from the hall that were sold after being decommissioned in 2018 as part of the revitalization project), the forty-seven-year-old passionate musicologist recalls a handful of his most cherished Massey experiences. Growing up in Rexdale in the 1970s, Stroumboulopoulos remembers

Morrissey played Massey Hall on September 12, 1997. It was a memorable show as the singer ended up getting kicked out, having been mistaken for one of the rowdy concertgoers.

taking the subway downtown and getting out at the Eaton Centre. He'd pause, look north on Yonge Street to where the neon signs swirled for music retailers Sam the Record Man and A&A Records, then walk south to Shuter to the legendary building. "I knew about Massey Hall and its mythology because of my Uncle Paul, who was always in our house playing his guitar and singing Gordon Lightfoot and Neil [Young] songs," Stroumboulopoulos says. "From an early age it always had this mystique for me ... and I remember wanting to see a show there."

One of his first times in the hallowed hall was in high school when he and some buddies went to see George Thorogood and the Destroyers, with the Razorbacks opening.

> Just walking into the place was so exciting. It wasn't just the room that was exciting, it was the process of how you got to the room. You would

get off that subway, walk through the Eaton Centre where you are in this world that doesn't even know there is a concert around the corner, and then suddenly you come through those doors and there it is. The room is so special. I feel context is important. If the audience is aware that the place is legendary and the artist is aware the place is legendary and both walk into the room with a little bit of deference to the history of the building, magic can happen there because then it is not about just another show. I've been to a lot of shows at Massey Hall and try not to take any of them for granted.

Debbie Harry, Blondie's co-founder, brought her band of punk and New Wave pioneers to Massey Hall in 1999 as part of their *No Exit* tour – the band's first live performance in sixteen years.

# CHAPTER 8

## The New Millennium

The 2000s kicked off with a pair of shows by Bryan Adams in January, Canadian comedy troupe Kids in the Hall performed three nights at the end of the month, and Jann Arden (who has now played the hall twenty-four times, the most of any Canadian woman performer and just one shy of Nana Mouskouri's total) hit the stage on June 2.

The decade also saw a fiftieth anniversary tribute to the famed "Greatest Jazz Concert Ever," which took place on May 15, 2003, and featured the quintet of Herbie Hancock, Roy Haynes, Roy Hargrove, Dave Holland, and Kenny Garrett. Max Roach, who, at seventy-nine, was the only surviving member of the original quintet, was led across the stage by Hancock before the band's encore. The crowd roared and rose to their feet. Feeling the reverberation of that incredible night in 1953, Roach told the crowd, "Charlie Parker and Mingus are

◂ Even before the revitalization enhanced the upper seats in the hall, no matter where you sat, you felt as if you could reach out and touch the performers on stage.

Herbie Hancock leads the Quintet's drummer, Max Roach, onto the stage during a 2003 commemoration concert of 1953's "Greatest Jazz Concert Ever."

here tonight. Things haven't changed. This is a great building for American music."[1]

Hancock himself had a similar reaction to Roach's. "I knew deeply about Massey Hall," he said, because he knew *Jazz at Massey Hall.* The record, he continued, "was so inspiring to so many musicians for so many decades that when I walked on the stage it was like a kind of spiritual reaction occurred in me, as though the spirit of that energy from that concert was still here."[2]

• • •

When Hart Massey gifted Massey Hall to the City of Toronto in 1894, his hope was that it would bring the community together and be a gathering place for generations to come. That vision of a broader

LIVE AT MASSEY HALL

## Various Artists, *Directions in Music: Live at Massey Hall*, 2002, Universal/Verve

*Directions in Music: Live at Massey Hall* is a live recording by Herbie Hancock, Roy Hargrove, and Michael Brecker recorded on October 25, 2001. The album was subtitled *Celebrating Miles Davis & John Coltrane*. The record won the 2003 Grammy for Best Jazz Instrumental Album, Individual or Group, and the track "My Ship" also won for Best Jazz Instrumental Solo that same year.

community connection carries on today in so many ways beyond the performances in this iconic building. When talk turns to the staff who have been fortunate to call Massey home, you realize that it, too, is a special community. It truly is a family affair. "You hear terms like work family thrown around a lot in corporate culture," says event coordinator Cal Woodruff. "It brings to mind outdated training videos and frighteningly perky, overbearing management, but at Massey Hall it is the genuine article. I was welcomed with open arms by a myriad of unique personalities into what I always describe as 'an island of misfit toys.'"

The new millennium brought a new generation of Massey Hall acolytes, partly thanks to concert promoters like Craig Laskey and Jeff Cohen, who presented their first show at the venue on June 14, 2006. The band: American indie rock outfit Bright Eyes, with Gillian Welch. The show occurred following years of Laskey and Cohen developing Conor Oberst and his band at smaller venues and clubs in the city. Presenting Bright Eyes at Massey was the logical next step in promoting the artist's career. Despite selling out the show, Cohen recalls how many lessons they learned from this first foray into a soft-seat concert hall:

(top) At twenty-four times, Jann Arden has played Massey Hall more than any woman artist except for Nana Mouskouri.

(bottom) Grammy-award winner Lenny Kravitz rocked Massey Hall on April 27, 2005, as part of his *Universal Love* tour.

Genre-bending music innovator Beck on stage with Wayne Coyne, lead singer of the Flaming Lips, on October 20, 2002.

> We were very nervous. First, we had no idea that anyone at Massey would take our phone call. Why would they want to deal with a bunch of punks? We were aware the Hall had a lot of rules … there are no rules in our world. We put in an offer and say you go on at this time, but that can move forty-five minutes either way; whatever happens, happens. We also controlled our ticketing. This was the first time we let someone else ticket a show for us. They also suggested we do some marketing and we were marketing-averse … we relied on word of mouth for most of our shows back then. I remember we got our first estimate back on the cost to just stage the show and it was like $18,500. We were used to a bill of $600! It was just really weird and a whole different world. We had no idea what we were doing. I don't even know why they let us in.

Despite Cohen and Laskey not knowing what they were doing, shows put on by Collective Concerts (the independent concert promotions company they founded in 2010) have been a regular occurrence at Shuter Street since that Bright Eyes concert. As Cohen says, they "punkified" the hall.

Current president and CEO Jesse Kumagai, who was the Director of Programming at the time, worked with them, helping with ticket pricing, and encouraged them to bring more shows to Massey. "[Kumagai] smoothed the pathway, rolled out the red carpet, and made us feel very comfortable there," says Cohen. Up until the venue closed for renovations in 2018, Collective Concerts presented more than forty shows at Massey Hall, including performances by Joel Plaskett, the Arkells, the National, the War on Drugs, Bon Iver, Sonic Youth, and Fleet Foxes. Laskey's favourite shows were a pair by Death Cab for Cutie on October 30–31, 2006. "For the Halloween show, they dressed up as Devo and did an entire set of Devo covers," he recalls. "I can't wait to promote shows there again."

• • •

Luke Doucet was one of the musicians who witnessed one of Young's three shows in November 2007. He shared the following story with the *Toronto Star*'s Ben Rayner:

> Seeing Neil Young at Massey Hall is a rite of passage for many of us. I play a reissue of a 1958 Gretsch White Falcon guitar and I play this guitar largely because it's what Neil used on

Country outlaw Willie Nelson stepped onto Massey Hall's stage for the first time on June 20, 2013. The legendary songwriter is seen here with harmonica whiz Mickey Raphael.

Bassist Kim Gordon of New York noisemakers Sonic Youth on stage during their final Toronto show on June 30, 2009.

> many of his iconic recordings before the early seventies, when he started to favour his famous black Les Paul. Since then, it has appeared only sporadically. For years, the only Neil song that Melissa [McClelland] and I ever played was "Winterlong," a somewhat obscure track that appeared, mysteriously, on *Decade*, primarily a compilation of singles. That first night I saw Neil at Massey Hall, I wasn't expecting to see the Falcon and I wasn't expecting him to play "Winterlong." When he sauntered out, mid-show, with his garish white wedding cake of a guitar, adorned with gold and ruby appointments, I figured I was seeing something rare. When he played the opening chords to "Winterlong," it was difficult for me not to feel like it was especially for me. It was one of the few times in my adult life that I had to remind myself of my robust atheism. For all of this to go down in the splendour of Massey Hall was an additional degree of poetry.[3]

George Stroumboulopoulos also attended one of those nights. "It felt like he had four hundred guitars on stage," he says. George recalls hearing "Helpless" and watching a musician who had the freedom to play what he wanted, not whatever the audience was calling out for.

• • •

For thirty-three years and counting, the Toronto Blues Society's (TBS) annual Women's Blues Revue has showcased some of the most accomplished women in the Canadian blues scene. Since its inception in 1987, the annual event has grown from a small gathering of society members at a small supper club at Portland and Queen streets in Toronto to a national showcase at Massey Hall. The Women's Blues Revue moved to Massey in 2004, where it found a permanent home for the next thirteen

SEMINAL SHOWS

## Neil Young, *Chrome Dreams II* Tour, November 2007

As a standing ovation greeted Neil Young each night on his return to Massey Hall for the first time since his 1973 show, many Toronto-area musicians were in the audience. The trio of concerts featured Neil playing a solo acoustic set, followed by an electric set backed by his wife, Pegi, as well as Ben Keith, Ralph Molina, and Rick Rosas.

years. The plan is to continue this showcase at Massey Hall when it reopens. It was apropos that this event would end up at Massey, since part of its mandate was to develop blues artists and bring them to a wider audience, which aligns with one of the hall's core strategic objectives. The formula, almost from day one, was to have six featured singers, which included a couple of headliners, all backed by a house band. Over the years it has featured more than a hundred different singers, including Rita Chiarelli, Serena Ryder, Shakura S'Aida, Suzie Vinnick, Divine Brown, and Sue Foley.

Shakura S'Aida grew up in Toronto's east end. She did not set foot in Massey Hall until attending concerts in her twenties and thirties when she splurged on tickets to see some of her idols, such as Mavis Staples and Lauryn Hill. Never once did she think that one day she might perform on that same stage, but it did offer hope. "Seeing Staples on that stage was a big moment," she recalls. "It allowed me to see there was a place for me and my community there." When the Women's Blues Revue moved to Massey, the songwriter seized the opportunity and fulfilled her dream of joining her heroes like Staples and Hill on that stage. Over the years since, she has participated in most of the annual blues showcases for women. Another highlight for her was opening for Grammy winner Keb' Mo' back in 2014. The blues maven hosted the final Women's Blues Revue at Massey Hall in 2017 before the event was moved to Roy Thomson Hall during the renovation closure.

It was no April Fool's joke: Belle & Sebastian fans got up close and personal when the Scottish band invited them on stage to dance at one point during the band's show on April 1, 2015.

Sue Foley, who grew up in Toronto but settled in Austin, Texas, in her early twenties, has opened for both B.B. King and Joe Cocker at Massey Hall, but her first performance there was as part of the Women's Blues Revue, the first year Massey hosted the event in 2004. "You don't know how beautiful it is until you are standing on the stage," she says. "The Women's Blues Revue is a celebration of women and great women musicianship. There is always a full house and it's a thrill to play in front of that many people. Hats off to the Toronto Blues Society. They are one of the main reasons Toronto has such a vibrant blues scene."

Another reason for Toronto's bustling blues scene is long-time Toronto promoter and arts consultant Derek Andrews. As one of the co-founders of the TBS, he's been involved since its inception. The idea for the

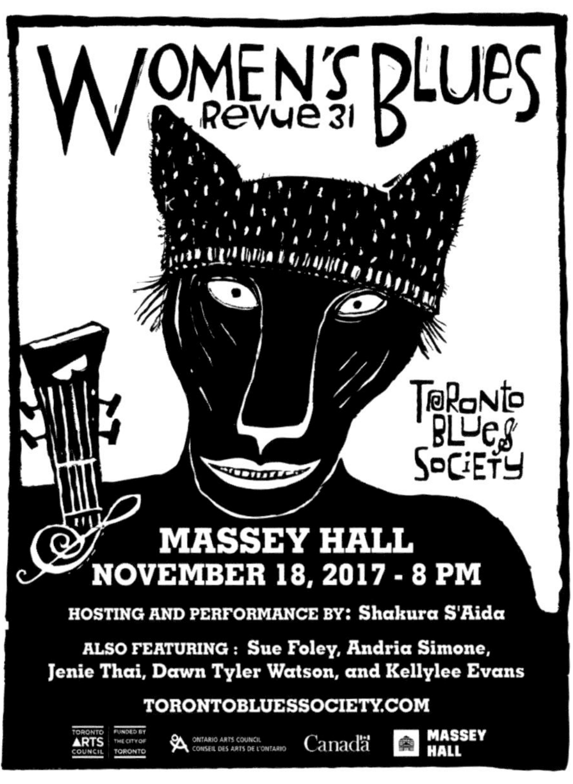

(left) A poster for the final Women's Blues Revue held at Massey Hall before the venue closed for renovations.

(right) On June 22, 2018, legendary blues and gospel singer Mavis Staples played songs from her deep catalogue, along with singing newer songs from her most recent record, *If All I Was Was Black*.

Women's Blues Revue came from a couple of board members, not long after the society was founded. Each year it gets bigger, better, and more successful. "It exceeded our expectations," he says. "It serves a demand [for] helping emerging artists at the beginning of their careers … and also [to] showcase established female blues singers."

As attendance grew to the point where they were selling out the Danforth Music Hall, Andrews chatted with Jesse Kumagai

> "Every single time I've been on that stage it has felt like home ... because of all of the artists who poured their sweat, blood, and tears onto that stage before you ... those layers are still there; you are walking on top of this energy that has been created by all these powerful musicians."
>
> — Shakura S'Aida, singer-songwriter

about next steps; Jesse suggested making the move to Massey. During the thirteen years before the venue closed for renovations, the program drew audiences of up to two thousand. "It's a Massey success story, as well," Andrews adds. "I've grown up in this city and love that venue. It's satisfying to produce in that hall a show that is so meaningful to the public."

In 2007, local indie band Rheostatics played their first farewell show at Massey Hall. The band had never headlined the venue before. "The irony that the Rheos' last performance would also happen there was not lost on my family, nor was the fact that, twenty-seven years earlier, my father had driven us to our first show a handful of blocks away at 102.1 the Edge," Dave Bidini recalled in his book *Around the World in 57.5 Gigs*. In fact, Bidini devoted an entire chapter in the book to Massey Hall.

"Tickets for the show sold fast," he writes. "Fans flew from across the country and drove hundreds of miles for this concert. The old hall looked beautiful from the stage. Its dark wooden ribbing absorbed whatever sounds we pushed from our amps. Because of the warmth of the venue and the love of the crowd, it was easy for us to connect despite our estrangement and the years of shit we'd forced on one another: stealing girlfriends and corrupting marriages, betraying trust, exploiting weaknesses, and saying absolutely the worst possible things.... At Massey Hall, the skies cleared and our hearts softened for a final time. In a way the show was like one long glorious apology to one another. We did two acoustic songs for our encore before saying goodbye. Everywhere I looked people were crying, and for the last verse and chorus of 'Record Body Count' they were both crying and singing. Afterward, there was a reception in Centuries bar downstairs for friends, family, and musical peers."

Singer-songwriter Molly Johnson grew up as a "theatre kid" in Toronto. From the age of five she was on the Royal Alexandra Theatre stage, performing along with her brother, Clark, in Mirvish musicals like *Porgy and Bess*, *South Pacific*, and *Finian's*

Sue Foley relaxes backstage. The Canadian musician, now based in Austin, Texas, played Massey Hall for the first time opening for B.B. King; she also participated for many years in the annual Women's Blues Revue presented by the Toronto Blues Society.

*Rainbow*, getting tips from Ed Mirvish himself. "We weren't a family that went to watch culture," says the JUNO award–winning jazz singer, songwriter, and Order of Canada recipient, "it was our job!" While the Royal Alexandra was more of a touchstone to her childhood, Massey Hall has been a constant in her adult years. Before booking and headlining her own gig at the venue for November 30, 2013 (with her

"First impressions: It just felt like (it) had this reverence to it – the way a lot of older halls [do] that weren't necessarily made for rock 'n' roll.... We sort of ... had to kick it back a notch for that room to get the most out of it. Light electric acoustic vibe ... it's best to not turn up too loud in that room."

– John Stirratt, bassist, Wilco

"The room is so special. I feel context is important. If the audience is aware that the place is legendary and the artist is aware the place is legendary and both walk into the room with a little bit of deference to the history of the building, magic can happen ..."

— George Stroumboulopoulos, radio host

Gord Downie on stage May 12, 2009, when he led his Tragically Hip bandmates through the first night of an epic six-evening run at Massey Hall.

long-time trio Robi Botos, Mike Downes, and Larnell Lewis), she had sung on the stage previously during multi-bill fundraising shows and as a backup singer for artists such as Tom Cochrane and Blue Rodeo. Like other hallowed halls in the world where she's performed, such as the Olympia in Paris, there is something intangible about playing what she calls "these old darlings."

"The ghosts that drift in and out and around you, like Edith Piaf at the Olympia, are ever-present and take your breath away just for a moment." Gordon Lightfoot, Canada's most revered songwriter, is one of those ghosts. Not now, but one day, his spirit will haunt Massey Hall. Artists fifty years from now will feel his soul when they step onto that stage, for no one has played the venue more than Mr. Lightfoot, as staff respectfully refer to him, who first stepped onto the stage as a teenager in the 1950s.

(top) The Rheostatics performed an emotional farewell show at the hall in 2007. The band later reunited for a show that was recorded as part of the hall's *Live at Massey Hall* concert film series on April 29, 2016.

(bottom) Tori Amos performed at Massey Hall on December 8, 2011, as part of her worldwide *Night of Hunters* tour.

EXIT

# CHAPTER 9

## The House of Gord

Canada Day 2018. It's Christmas in July for Gordon Lightfoot. The country turns 151. Lightfoot, seventy-nine at the time, enters the stage door off Shuter Street to play the hall he can rightfully call home. It's the third of three sold-out nights before the hall closes for extensive renovations. Long-time friends saying adieu for a few years — a hall and a performer — intertwined over the course of more than a half-century. It's 2:00 p.m. A few people gather with vinyl copies of *Sundown* and *Old Dan's Records*. The songwriter pauses, smiles, and says hello; then he signs an LP or two to the worshippers' delight. Many have made the pilgrimage year after year to hear Gord play at his favourite venue. The stage door closes, and he shuffles down the short flight of stairs, his steps a little more measured, a little slower than the first time he made this trek in 1967. Lightfoot heads to his dressing

◂ Gordon Lightfoot performs on Canada Day, 2018, to a sold-out crowd.

Crowds gather outside Massey Hall before Lightfoot's sold-out show on Canada Day, July 1, 2018.

room; it's a space as familiar and comfortable as his Rosedale living room. Sound check and a two-hour rehearsal follows. Gord is a perfectionist. "In a way, playing there was always a challenge," he explains. "You had to be sure the intonation was correct on all the instruments. You had to be locked in with the keyboards. We work on that for two to three hours before a show."

Later, as the performer is getting loose and ready backstage, Centuries bar downstairs is aflutter: Couples toast the occasion with Prosecco. Buddies sip beers and soak in all the memorabilia lining the walls. Some gaze in wonder at all the photos of the performers who have stood on the stage above them over the last 124 years. They also silently wonder what the hall will look like

"There are lots of great concert halls in the world. They are just different; one isn't better than the other. Massey Hall is important because it's ours. It's a forgiving, beautiful, and inspiring place."

— Dave Bidini, Rheostatics

Gordon Lightfoot was the last person to play Massey Hall (June 29, June 30, and July 1, 2018) before the venue closed for over three years as part of its revitalization project.

when it reopens. Lightfoot fans, young and old, mix and mingle. Some are dressed up. Some are dressed down. The constant: there are smiles all around. They know they're in for a special evening and feel lucky to be there to witness and share in such a significant Massey memory.

An hour later, upstairs, a standing ovation from the sold-out audience greets Lightfoot as he ambles across the wooden floor from stage left with the four members of his long-time backing band. He's wearing a burgundy velvet jacket, white dress shirt, and black pants. A who's who of the Canadian music industry is in the house. People have made the pilgrimage from far and wide. Jim Cuddy and his family sit a dozen rows back. Spotted elsewhere are boxer George Chuvalo, dozens of other musicians, and Lightfoot's friends and extended family.

Gord looks at the audience gathered in the "pews," gazing from the floor to the upper galleries before launching into "Now and Then" — doing what he has done more than 165 times over the preceding decades: delivering a sermon of songs in his church. He creates a spiritual event and provides joy as he has done each time he has performed on the hallowed stage.

He waits for the applause to subside, and then, with a deadpan delivery, says, "I am Gordon Lightfoot and the reports of my death have been greatly exaggerated."

Two sets and twenty-six songs from his extensive and growing catalogue later — from "The Wreck of the Edmund Fitzgerald" to "Carefree Highway," "Early Morning Rain" to "Sundown" — plus a one-song encore ("Cold on Your Shoulder"), the Minister of Music has closed the hall for a three-year period. The audience sang along to each song. There was laughter. There were tears. There was plenty of joy. Even the ghosts clapped and sang along.

At one point our national musical muse/hero said, "Oh these hallowed boards. The hall still stands."

Yes, Gord, thank God it still does.

Lightfoot's courtship with Massey Hall began when he was a child. Growing up in Orillia, Ontario, he showed early on that he had a gift for music, singing at weddings and at ladies' auxiliary meetings from the time he was twelve. He was destined to one day not only play the country's most famed venue, but become as legendary as the hall is to the cultural fabric of Canada.

Flash back to 1951. That's when, as a young teen, Lightfoot first set foot on this storied stage. The young lad had travelled down the highway from his hometown to perform in a singing competition as part of the ninth annual Stars of the Festival Kiwanis concert, which showcased all of the winners in various age categories. "Massey Hall was a big one for me," says Lightfoot. "To get in there at thirteen and stand up on that stage at that age, it never left me."

Lightfoot was a soprano. He had won his class competition so earned the opportunity to compete as part of this two-night showcase. "You had to get really good at the tune you were doing," Lightfoot recalls, speaking one evening from his Rosedale home. "I would practise for weeks going into the competition. My song was called 'Who Is Sylvia?' The place was packed with mothers, teachers, people from the Royal Conservatory and various Kiwanis clubs. I got out there and did my tune. One thing I remember the most from the whole experience was a kid on that show who played the clarinet; he was about sixteen or seventeen years old and I had never heard anybody play the clarinet like that — before or since. It never left me. It was the highlight of the whole thing. After that, my dad took us to one of the big fancy Chinese restaurants downtown."

Lightfoot returned to Massey Hall four years later as a member of a barbershop quartet. They were part of an extravaganza that also featured the Buffalo Bills — one of the great barbershop groups. "We got on the front end of one of their shows," the songwriter recalls.

A brief appearance in the early sixties as part of a hootenanny show produced by musicologist Oscar Brand followed, but the songwriter would not return again for nearly a decade. Instead, he would first hone his songs and his craft in the coffee houses of Yorkville, north of Massey Hall. Before he earned a place in the Yorkville scene, Lightfoot built a following at the Steeles Tavern, an iconic venue on Yonge Street located between Sam the Record Man and A&A Records, just north of Massey Hall. It's here that the young songwriter first bonded with local singer Ronnie Hawkins; the pair discovered they shared a love of music and women.

Once Lightfoot tested out his original songs and gained more confidence, he moved on from the Steeles Tavern to regular gigs in the coffee houses of Yorkville, playing for ten times the money.

In 1967, Lightfoot's promoter Bernie Fiedler knew the time was right for the legendary performer to have his first solo show at Massey Hall. The performer's debut album (*Lightfoot!*) had come out in the United States on Warner Bros. Records the previous year and was doing well on the strength of some of his best-loved compositions: "For Lovin' Me," "Early Morning

(top) Before Lightfoot played Massey Hall, he played regularly in Yorkville in the mid- to late 1960s at coffee shops like the Riverboat. Here, he chats outside the venue in early January 1967 with artist Robert Markle on the first night of a month-long residency.

(bottom) Lightfoot, as seen at his home in 1965, playing guitar.

The *Toronto Telegram* advertises Lightfoot's Massey Hall solo debut on March 31, 1967.

Rain," "Steel Rail Blues," and "Ribbon of Darkness." The twenty-eight-year-old Lightfoot earned approximately five thousand dollars for his first solo appearance at Massey Hall. It's apropos that Canada's most treasured songwriter would make his solo Massey Hall debut during the country's centennial. A critic for the *Globe and Mail* at the time described the show as a "country-and-Lightfoot parade of Canadiana."[1]

From this debut, Lightfoot started a tradition of playing a run of shows at the hall every year. In 1978, he broke his own record, playing ten sold-out shows in nine days.

> We were doing so well in Yorkville at the clubs such as the Purple Onion and the Riverboat, we figured we would give Massey Hall a shot. Lo and behold we started to get ticket sales. It was one night at first! We did really well. I went in with a trio: [me], Red Shea, and John Stockfish. We were really honking it out in those days. It worked out, so we started doing it every year. Then we increased it to twice. Then we did it three times, until we had done it like twenty-five times in twenty-five years, and I said, "We better cut this back to half that." I was starting to feel like a tulip coming up in a little old lady's garden!

After the stage lights went down and the last encore was sung at most of these concerts, Lightfoot and his band would retreat to Massey's dressing rooms, holding court with friends and family, sharing beers and laughs. Often, the party would continue into the next day at Lightfoot's Rosedale mansion.

This trend of playing Massey every other year continued for the next four decades. It's not surprising that Lightfoot holds the record for the most appearances at the

On November 26, 2014, Charles Cutts, Massey Hall's president and CEO at the time, joined Elizabeth Dowdeswell, the lieutenant governor of Ontario, to present the seventy-six-year-old Lightfoot with the first-ever Massey Hall Honours Award.

hall by any solo artist with more than 165 shows under his belt. His booking became so successful at the Shuter Street venue that its main tenant for years, the Toronto Symphony Orchestra, was forced to book its vacations around Lightfoot's annual residencies. Beyond his many shows, the JUNO award winner has recorded a pair of albums at Massey (*Sunday Concert*, 1969, and *All Live*, 2012).

What Lightfoot, like the majority of artists and fans, loves the most about the iconic venue are the acoustics. "The place has got a sound like no other hall that I know of in all of North America," he explains. "I can tell you that honestly. It's completely different. Most of them sound the same as a matter of fact, but Massey Hall has a different sound of any hall I have ever played in, and that includes places over in the U.K."

On nights when Lightfoot was not holding court centre stage at Massey, or on the road, you often found him in the venue, watching the symphony, Dave Brubeck, Pavarotti, or other Canadian artists who revered him and who he had struck up friendships with, such as singer-songwriter Ron Sexsmith.

Lightfoot, during the 1970s, on the stage he calls his second home.

Lightfoot says what also makes Massey so special to him is that, since it's a hometown show, he knows when he looks out into that audience there will be many familiar faces looking back. "All your friends are going to be in the audience, so you want to make sure you do a really good job," he adds. "Whenever you go to Massey Hall, you have to perform the greatest show possible."

Sexsmith was lucky to befriend the legendary songwriter early in his career. Before that, he was a fan, just like everyone else. Even before moving to Toronto, he would make the trek to the city to see Lightfoot play. Sexsmith attended his first show in the mid-eighties. "I was aware that Gord playing Massey was a bit of a tradition, and around that time, shortly after my son was born, I was just becoming a real fan of his, and also of Leonard Cohen, as I figured out what kind of songwriter I was going to be. Lightfoot came on strong."

In 1987, Sexsmith moved to Toronto, allowing him to see one of his songwriting heroes play the venue regularly. "I never missed a show," he says. "I was working in the downtown core as a foot courier. I would pass Massey Hall every day; it was a place I could not see myself ever filling, but it didn't seem impossible to play there ... I thought maybe I could get there."

From that moment forward, the musician vowed that he would not play the church on Shuter Street until he could headline the venue. Sexsmith eventually did just that at forty-two years of age on April 8, 2006. Was he nervous? Definitely. "That first time getting on that stage it felt like I was sleepwalking a bit ... it was like a crazy dream," he remembers.

The songwriter arrived at noon to soak up every single second of the experience, spending time in the dressing room, trying on different clothes, figuring out what to wear on stage. Then, right before he was set to go on, Lightfoot showed up. Sexsmith heard the roar from the crowd as his songwriting hero walked to his seat. If he had nerves before he knew Lightfoot was in the crowd, those jitters jumped up a few levels. "Everything became loftier for me," Sexsmith admits. "The first time I went to pick up my glass of water, my hands were shaking."

Massey Hall and Gord have that effect on people. Both command respect and both elicit nervous energy. Just ask Barry Keane. When Lightfoot's long-time drummer, who was first hired by the songwriter in 1972 as a studio musician to play on *Old Dan's Records*, was asked for one of his

Lightfoot looks over the setlist in his "house" prior to a show in 1996.

At more than 165 times, Lightfoot's record of playing Massey Hall surpasses everyone else's by far.

most significant Massey Hall moments, he said the one that sticks out the most is not the first concert he played there, but rather his audition there not long after that initial meeting.

> At the time, Gord was kicking around the idea of adding a drummer to his live shows and asked me if I would be interested in the gig. I said sure, of course. And, believe it or not, the next thing I knew he had rented out Massey Hall to see what it would be like to play there with a drummer. Imagine how intimidating it was for me? Here I was on an empty stage in an empty hall with Gordon Lightfoot playing six-string and twelve-string

guitar, singing un-miked, playing un-miked, with Rick Haynes on electric bass, Terry Clements on acoustic guitar, and me on full set of drums. I was basically being auditioned in that circumstance. I will never forget that at one point, Gord, turning to face me, came back to the drums.... giving me a solo performance of "If You Could Read My Mind" and testing me out ... I'll never forget that! That was the first time I ever played on the Massey Hall stage ... apparently, it went okay!

As part of the fiftieth anniversary JUNOs broadcast on CBC, Gordon Lightfoot introduced the Tragically Hip — the first band to play in the newly named Allan Slaight Auditorium.

Besides the trio of appearances to close Massey Hall in July, Lightfoot played seventy-five shows in other venues in 2018. This endurance from an eighty-year-old is truly remarkable. When Massey Hall announced its reopening plans in the summer of 2021, it was no surprise that Lightfoot was to play the first three nights (November 25–27). For as the late Deane Cameron (Massey Hall president and CEO from 2015 to 2019) often quipped, "Gord is our musical patriarch and boss!"

"If you want to make a statement in Toronto, say you've arrived in the city, you are for real, and you have a story to tell, the best conduit to communicate that story is Massey Hall."

— Riley O'Connor, chair, Live Nation Canada

STAGE DOOR

# CHAPTER 10

## Last Call at the Hall

When two passionate artists collide with like-minded visions, the result is a magical piece of filmmaking — art for art's sake. This sums up Academy Award–winning director Jonathan Demme's rock documentary *Neil Young Journeys*, which premiered at the Toronto International Film Festival on September 12, 2011, before seeing a broader release the following year. Part road movie, part concert documentary, *Journeys* chronicled a pair of Neil's shows at Massey Hall in May 2011, when he was touring to promote *Le Noise*, the record he made with producer Daniel Lanois. This was the third documentary collaboration between Young and Demme, as the two had previously teamed up for *Neil Young: Heart of Gold* (2006) and *Neil Young Trunk Show* (2009).

The film begins with Neil giving viewers a tour of Omemee, Ontario — a locale where he spent several of his formative years — in a 1956 Ford Crown Victoria. The nostalgic tour done, the car leaves Omemee and these memories

◂ In the summer of 2018, the last performing artists left through the alleyway stage door as the hall shut for revitalization.

# Neil Young, *Honour the Treaties* Tour, January 12, 2014

Neil Young's last performance at Massey Hall was on a Sunday night in January as part of the *Honour the Treaties* tour, a series of benefit concerts that also featured Diana Krall, to raise money for a legal fight against the expansion of the Athabasca oil sands.

Tragically Hip frontman Gord Downie was there that night, and he spoke to journalist Nick Patch about the meaningful experience:

> I was crying very hot tears the whole show. [...] It was my Neil Young jukebox, one after the other. But then it was the confluence of a lot of things. Like [...] how much I admired his courage and how laggard this country has been for that courage. [...] It was so powerful and it's been so missing. I'll always be grateful for that night, for Neil Young.[1]

All in the family: Massey Hall staff pose outside the venue on July 1, 2018, before the Gordon Lightfoot show that evening.

behind, and heads down the highway to Toronto and his Massey Hall dates.

The concert footage shows Young performing most of the numbers from *Le Noise*, along with classics such as "Ohio," "Down by the River," "After the Gold Rush," and "Hey Hey, My My." The mercurial musician moves between two pianos, an organ, and several of his famed electric guitars: his Gretsch White Falcon, his customized Gibson Les Paul Goldtop (known as Old Black), and other classic acoustics. Demme's deft directing ensures every passionate note and nuance from Neil's instruments are noticed.[2]

• • •

Hart Massey gifted Massey Hall to the City of Toronto as a place "for the people." This story shows how, more than a century after it opened, the hall remains true to Massey's mandate. It is a place where anyone with the wherewithal, desire, and determination can spend one night on that storied stage.

November 17, 2010, is a day etched in Andrea Freedman Iscoe's memory. That is the night she fulfilled a lifelong dream of playing Massey Hall. What makes this story unique is that Iscoe is not a professional

Iggy Pop, along with his Stooges bandmates, took to Massey Hall's stage on August 6, 2008, for an unforgettable performance.

> "In my first year, my favourite rock star, Iggy Pop, came with the Stooges … and at one point, without warning, he invited the audience on stage. They proceeded to play two songs with hundreds of patrons jumping around him; it was amazing and terrifying."
>
> – Cal Woodruff, Massey Hall event coordinator and long-time employee

musician. She is not a promoter. Nor was she ever part of the music industry. Her journey to the hall started in the 1960s when she *was* a musician and dreamed of performing there, but marriage, kids, and, as they say, life, put those aspirations on hold. Then, in 2010, she hosted "A Night at Massey Hall" — a benefit concert she organized for SOS Children's Villages Canada. The event not only fulfilled her dream of stepping onto the storied stage, but also provided the same opportunity for a cast of one hundred others who took part: from veteran professional musicians like Little Caesar and the Consuls to performers that by day cut hair, were busy studying, or led a congregation in prayer.

Flash back to 2008, when a friend approached Iscoe about helping organize a fundraiser for the charity SOS Children's Villages. She told her she'd be happy to help, but that if they were going to do it, she wanted to "go big or go home!" She didn't want to do this in a community centre basement. "Why not Massey Hall?" she thought. She then called, put down a deposit, and booked a date two years away — November 17, 2010. Iscoe says she choose that date for its significance. "It was the day my late mother was born and also the date my best friend's mother died."

The show took two years to put together, and Iscoe solicited musicians via a casting call on Craigslist. "I figured if I wanted to perform at Massey Hall, there must be many others with the same dream." She put up an ad that said, "I'm holding a concert at Massey Hall and looking for singers and musicians to join me." People started calling her immediately and she went out to hear people sing and play in bars all over the city. "A mother even called me from British Columbia about a band that included two of her sons. They ended up joining the event. It's a testament to how badly people want to perform there."

She also called the Claude Watson School for the Arts and invited a number of their students to dance. In the end, she got more than one hundred people involved. "I created bands and Duff Roman



## Justin Bieber, *Home for the Holidays*, December 21, 2011

Justin Bieber performed a surprise concert at Massey Hall, a Christmas TV taping titled *Home for the Holidays*. The concert, which sold out in less than thirty minutes (eBay listed a front-row single for $1,999), aired on MuchMusic and CTV throughout the 2011 holiday season. All proceeds from the concert went to Bieber's Believe charity.[3]

Jesse Kumagai, president and CEO of Massey Hall, says they only had a few days' notice that the concert was happening. "It was the first time in a long time we had an artist of that scale come in on such short notice. Everyone had to drop everything. It was a remarkable exercise in what the global impact of a superstar is.... There were thousands of Bieber fans on Shuter Street. When we opened the door, for a fraction of a second I felt what it would be like to be Justin Bieber. I put earplugs in before the show started to drown out the screaming." Katie Beaton, who was working as an usher that night, adds, "The screams actually shook the walls of the old Albert Building next door!"

helped me audition the acts and acted as the emcee for the night." They ended up selling 1,500 tickets. "My theory was that the more people I had in the show, the more families that would attend, and it worked. Everybody who participated volunteered his or her time. I promised all the performers that their name with a brief bio would [appear] in the program.

"It was awesome! Walking on stage for the first time when I was meeting with the Massey Hall staff made me feel like a kid in a candy store. This was my dream."

Iscoe and her team ended up raising $25,000, enough to support a house in Canada's first fully funded SOS Children's Village in Ondangwa, Namibia, which they named A Night at Massey Hall House. She says that many people donated beyond their ticket price. Sponsors also helped to offset some of the operating costs, and Iscoe herself paid for many of the other services such as lighting rental. "This was my first leap into producing a concert, and it was an education. I had so little time to practise my own songs, but when my turn came to perform, I sang 'The House of the Rising Sun' and 'Summertime.' I remember walking on stage and I was not nervous, I don't know why. It just felt like home. I'm really happy I did it. It certainly was a place for the people that night."

• • •

In 2016, Canadian comedian Russell Peters recorded a Netflix special at Massey Hall. Peters, who was born in Toronto and grew up in Brampton, Ontario, had spent two years performing 250 shows across 120 cities and 25 countries. The comedian ended this globetrotting *Almost Famous* world tour with two nights at Toronto's legendary venue. "I wanted to do it in my city," he said, "and I think Massey Hall defines my city."[4]

Massey Hall has a tradition of celebrating Canadian songwriters. In 2013, it was Joni Mitchell's turn. She had not toured since 2000 and had rarely even been seen in public during that time, but somehow Jörn Weisbrodt, artistic director of the Luminato Festival, came up with the idea to celebrate the beloved singer with a birthday party and coaxed her to attend.

Originally, Mitchell was not interested, but after a series of calls she warmed to the idea and suggested Brian Blade as music director. The pair met in person and started a friendship. At a dinner party hosted by the actress Carrie Fisher, following dinner and some libations, Mitchell recited a new poem she had written; Rufus Wainwright (Weisbrodt's partner) said Joni should recite it on stage at Massey Hall. The seed was planted. Weisbrodt says he never pushed

"Massey Hall was the only place where this show should have taken place. Massey Hall has this grit to it. You could mess with this space. There was always something that attracted me to it; it had this line back into the past. You knew a lot of great things had happened there."

— Jörn Weisbrodt, artistic director, Luminato Festival

her to come to Luminato, but on her own she started to get excited about the Toronto event in her honour.

The surprise came at the end of the evening when Mitchell stepped to the microphone, having not performed in public for many years. The crowd was delirious. Mitchell first recited "Rain," a poem she had written, which was inspired by Emily Carr, then sang a pair of songs ("Furry Sings the Blues" and "Don't Interrupt the Sorrow") before joining the rest of the guests who had feted her in a closing rendition of "Woodstock."

Weisbrodt says, "She sang. That was a moment. The audience freaked out. Afterwards, backstage in one of the big dressing rooms, it was so beautiful. Atom Egoyan and his wife [Arsinée Khanjian] were there and we had a big birthday cake for [Joni]. I still have vivid memories of that time."

Bill King — musician, photographer, radio host, and music lover — was there that night with his camera, ready to capture the historic moment. King admits he is not nostalgic by nature, but on this night, he allowed himself the luxury. "While sitting at Massey Hall and devouring the three-hour plus celebration, I couldn't help but return to

Canada's song-poet Joni Mitchell gives an unexpected performance during the Luminato Festival in her honour on June 18, 2013.

those crowded streets in Greenwich Village in the 1960s — the tourists, the hippies, the musicians, and the excitement: a place where Dylan was expected at the Gaslight, Mingus was around the corner, and the Mothers of Invention were across the way."

King got word Mitchell would be singing near the end; he waited with his camera in his bag, hoping to find his chance.

> I had no plan other than to embrace the occasion and hopefully catch the last departing images. When Mitchell recited "Rain," it was a near out-of-body experience much like the song that followed — "Furry Sings the Blues." It's that rhythmic slam of a beat poet — the rap most rappers can never employ. The dialogue that spits and bites — dances, embraces, lets go — all the while striking all sides the beat. As good as those who stood on stage and sang were — and they sang their hearts out — Mitchell stood on moving clouds.

When Mitchell left the stage, the audience broke into "Happy Birthday," even though the actual day wasn't for another four months. The singer returned, took

Spirit of the West played an emotional concert on June 6, 2015. It was the Canadian band's first time headlining Massey and one of the final performances by lead singer John Mann, who died of Alzheimer's in 2019.

one final bow, and simply said, "This is so much fun."

Rufus Wainwright was one of the performers celebrating Mitchell that evening. The singer-songwriter had headlined the hall three years earlier (December 3, 2003), but for the son of Loudon Wainwright III and Kate McGarrigle, this tribute to Joni stands out as one of the greatest nights.[5] "I stayed after the show until 4:00 a.m. backstage, just jamming, drinking, and exchanging items of clothing," Wainwright recalls. "I gave her my sparkly scarf; we will leave it at that! There were a lot of hugs that night. That will always remain in my memory as one of the great, great evenings of my musical career: just Joni, me, Jörn, and Glen Hansard serenading her, and her just lapping it up."

June 6, 2015, is another date now etched into the patina of Massey Hall's walls. For on that night, Vancouver's Spirit of the West, after a thirty-year career, finally headlined the venue for the first time. That is not what made this show so special, however. The concert was bittersweet for another reason: it was the farewell to fans for the band's lead singer John Mann, who was diagnosed in 2014, when he was only fifty-two, with Alzheimer's disease. The love in the air and respect for Mann and his bandmates that night was palpable. The band had played a gig in London, Ontario, two nights before, where Mann struggled. With a day off in Toronto before the Massey show, Spirit of the West rehearsed acoustically in their hotel room. To say on the day of the show they were all nervous is an understatement. It's one thing to play the country's most iconic venue for the first time, but imagine doing that when your lead singer has Alzheimer's and what will happen next is unpredictable. Geoffrey Kelly, multi-instrumentalist and one of the band's principal song writers along with Mann, took over the emcee duties that night. To help John remember the lyrics, they had an iPad that bass player Tobin Frank scrolled for him with a foot pedal. John rose to the occasion and there was not a dry eye in the building as the band played hits such as "And If Venice Is Sinking," "Political," and their party-anthem "Home for a Rest." Recalling this magical evening more than five years later, and following Mann's passing in November 2019, still gives Kelly a warm feeling.

> It just happened John had a great night. In front of our peers, our friends, and our families, it was a glorious night and a triumphant performance by John. It's like he sensed the importance of the occasion and he delivered the goods. It

"The three Gords" backstage. On February 2, 2017, Gord Downie (left), after giving his final public performance on Massey's stage at a Blue Rodeo show, was joined by Gordon Lightfoot and Canadian actor/director Gordon Pinsent (right).

was such a special gig. Massey Hall was packed and there was so much support from the audience … they were like a safety net; everyone knew what John was going through. It felt electric! I never sensed that kind of support anywhere else away from the Commodore Ballroom in Vancouver. I'll treasure that memory forever.

"Massey Hall is just one of those places. It raises your game; your genes vibrate at a different level and you feel the presence of all the great artists that have performed there on that old stage."

— Greg Keelor, Blue Rodeo

Another seminal moment took place on February 2, 2017, when the Tragically Hip's beloved singer, Gord Downie, gave his final public performance on the Massey stage, joining Blue Rodeo and the Sadies in a rendition of Blue Rodeo's hit song "Lost Together." Greg Keelor, co-founder of Blue Rodeo, shared with me his memories from that night, when not just one famous Canadian "Gord," but three, were in the hall.

That night, "The night of the three Gords," was beyond! To know

Gordon Lightfoot, Gordon Pinsent, and Gord Downie were in the audience made it so special. When Gord Downie came onstage with Dallas and Travis Good [from the Sadies] for the encore of "Lost Together," it was like this wave of love and joy filled the hall. Gord was a beam of light then — "the man who walks with stars" — he had assumed the mantle and he wore it with inspiring dignity. Travis did his verse, Dallas did his, and then Gord sang in tongues and it was all understood.

Over the years, Massey Hall has hosted numerous award ceremonies, fundraisers, and multi-artist events, from the annual Dream Serenade benefit concerts to celebrate and support children with exceptionalities and their caregivers that started in 2013, to the annual Women's Blues Revue. But none can match the star-studded event held on September 23, 2017, when the Canadian Songwriters Hall of Fame inducted four new members: Québécois band Beau Dommage, songwriter Stéphane Venne, and singers/songwriters/activists Bruce Cockburn and Neil Young.

Highlights of the evening included several musical tributes. Young was honoured with a performance by Randy Bachman,

(top) William Prince (left) and Bruce Cockburn backstage after the Canadian Songwriters Hall of Fame induction ceremony on September 23, 2017. Earlier in the evening, Prince paid tribute to the legendary musician, performing a stirring version of Cockburn's "Stolen Land."

(bottom) On August 4, 2016, as part of the third season of the *Live at Massey Hall* series, Peaches gave a frenzied and sexually charged performance.

## Blue Rodeo, *Live at Massey Hall*, 2015, Warner Music

Blue Rodeo have played Massey more than any other band – thirty-six times. Hometown shows at the hall were always special. Released by Warner Music Canada on October 16, 2015, the album was recorded in 2014 during their tour for the album *In Our Nature*.[6] "Blue Rodeo are so synonymous with Toronto, and with Massey, it always felt like the perfect marriage," said Steve Kane, president of Warner Music Canada. "Offhand, they said they had taped the last show at Massey the previous February. From the minute we started to listen, you could feel the ambience and feel the hall in this record."

Canadian singer-songwriter Emily Haines (Metric, Broken Social Scene) made her solo debut at Massey Hall with her band the Soft Skeleton on December 5, 2017.

who told stories about his long-time friend and played a medley of acoustic songs. Later, Bachman joined the Arkells for an electric rendition of Young's "Rockin' in the Free World." After an acoustic take on "Old Man," Whitehorse jammed out on "Ohio" and k.d. lang sang a stunning cover of the songwriter's classic song "Helpless."

Cradling his trademark Gretsch White Falcon guitar, Luke Doucet realized a life-long dream of playing in front of one of his musical heroes.

> Neil sat in the third row and stared at us while we played his songs … I felt to honour Neil's legacy as an artist you needed to acknowledge his contribution to the electric guitar … and I was well-positioned to make some noise on my instrument as someone who Neil had a massive influence on. Playing in front of Neil was terrifying, inspiring, and cathartic. A couple of months later, we received a letter from Neil thanking us. Then, he added, "by the way Luke, you really nailed Stephen's guitar parts!" I thought it was hilarious. That guitar in "Ohio" is so inspiring and I would have said it's quintessentially Neil, but apparently a lot of those licks were Stephen Stills's. Who cares? I got to play for Neil! And, that was special.

## Burton Cummings, *Massey Hall*, 2012, Universal

"I'm thrilled to have done an album there. It now makes me a part of the patchwork quilt of its history," says Burton Cummings. "I called the record *Massey Hall*, not *Burton Cummings Live at Massey Hall*, so I guess I'm a little bit part of that history."

"I still love that album," Cummings adds, when asked to recall the live record seven years later. "I think we did two nights and picked the best versions from the two nights. The response was tremendous; we filmed a part of it. On some of the danceable songs like 'Albert Flasher' and 'My Own Way to Rock' — a lot of girls got up and paraded down the aisles."

Buffy Sainte-Marie joins Whitehorse as part of the hall's 124th birthday concert.

That same night, Blackie and the Rodeo Kings also paid tribute to Bruce Cockburn, playing one of his more politically charged numbers, "If I Had a Rocket Launcher." And singer-songwriter William Prince was joined by Inuk singer Elisapie for a duet on Cockburn's "Stolen Land," which on this night was a timely reminder of the plight of Indigenous Peoples in this country and how far we still have to go when it comes to reconciliation.

One of the final multi-performance events at the venue before its temporary closure was billed as "Celebrating Massey Hall," in honour of the hall's 124th birthday (June 14, 2018). The concert boasted an all-Canadian lineup that featured performances by Jim Cuddy, Sarah Harmer, Leah Fay and Peter Dreimanis of July Talk, Joel Plaskett, Sam Roberts, and Buffy Sainte-Marie. Massey Hall darlings Whitehorse acted as both the house band and a feature act on this memorable night.

# CHAPTER 11

## Revitalization

There must be something spiritual in Massey Hall's foundation. Maybe before Hart Massey passed, he uttered a prayer that would protect his gift for generations. Or perhaps his Methodist spirit, serving as the hall's eternal guardian, still lurks in the walls, ensuring they are never torn down or changed dramatically from the philanthropist's original vision. Whatever the reason, while Toronto's skyline has shifted and neighbouring tenants have come and gone, through recessions, depressions, and the demolition of other local heritage sites, for over 127 years Massey Hall has stood the test of time. What is certain is that the hall would not have survived without some facelifts.

When the population of the city rapidly expanded, bringing with it more traffic and larger crowds, necessary changes were required to keep Massey Hall functional and relevant. From the first major touch-ups in the early 1900s, when the venue was less than a decade old, to the major revitalization that began in

◂ Original stained glass lovingly restored and now visible for the first time in over a century.

Scaffolding fills the auditorium to allow restorers access to the scalloped ceiling.

2018, requiring the venue's closure for more than three years, ongoing renewal helped keep the doors open while enhancing this iconic performing and listening space.

From 1949 until the 2000s, few changes were made to the building. In 1955, the ceiling started to crumble, and a large chunk of plaster fell onto the floor, luckily when the hall was empty. Rather than fix the plaster properly, management installed wire mesh as a low-cost solution to cover up this structural problem. One of the major additions was the installation of air conditioning, financed and necessitated in 1989 by the arrival of Andrew Lloyd Webber's Broadway musical *Cats*, which rented out the hall for nine months of performances. This addition allowed the venue to book shows in the hot, humid summer months. Finally, to coincide with the hall's centennial in 1994, the basement was refurbished and a bar (Centuries) was added.

"It's a remarkable acoustic hall and unique in the world. There is no place like it. When they built the Sydney Opera House in Australia, they sent engineers here to find out everything about Massey Hall so they could emulate it."
— David Clayton-Thomas, Blood, Sweat & Tears

Centuries, the much-loved basement bar, remains as part of the multi-million-dollar facelift, but also gets a refresh.

By the time the twenty-first century arrived, Massey Hall, which had been designated a National Historic Site in 1981, was long overdue for a facelift to fix a multitude of structural issues and add the modern amenities and conveniences expected by today's patrons — extra washrooms, more comfortable seating, elevators to make the hall more accessible. One of the main stumbling blocks to fulfilling any of this was a lack of space. That changed in 2012 when Tricon Capital and MOD Developments acquired a plot of land on Yonge Street that included the 450-square-metre lot immediately behind Massey Hall and generously transferred the land to the Corporation of Massey Hall and Roy Thomson Hall.

Finally, the corporation had the extra space they needed to make significant changes. Immediately, they drafted a long-term strategic plan and sought support from the municipal, provincial, and federal governments. With a plan to seek funds from private philanthropists and corporate donors and the broad Massey Hall community of long-time subscribers and patrons, an ambitious two-phase, $139-million revitalization project was supported by Toronto City

"[Massey Hall] is not the most beautiful venue, but it is the most magical venue. I think now, with the revitalization, it will also become the most beautiful venue. It is just so beloved."

— Molly Johnson, blues musician

Council, the City of Toronto's Heritage Preservation Board, city staff, and the Ontario Heritage Trust.

"Change Nothing, Improve Everything" was the slogan that guided the hall during the most recent renovations.

KPMB Architects led the restoration and renovation. The Toronto firm is an award-winning and internationally recognized design company responsible for projects like Koerner Hall and the TELUS Centre for Performance and Learning, both part of the Royal Conservatory of Music in Toronto. KPMB founding partner Marianne McKenna brought to Massey Hall a special focus on the architecture of concert halls and on how design can be used to engage community. She was supported in her efforts by the architects at Goldsmith Borgal & Company Ltd. Architects (GBCA), a Toronto-based firm specializing in the restoration, rehabilitation, and adaptive reuse of heritage buildings, and by renowned acoustician Bob Essert, the founding director of Sound Space Vision, who has more than thirty-five years' experience and over 150 projects to his credit, including the Canadian Opera Company's Four Seasons Centre for the Performing Arts.

"Don't mess with the sound!" was the common refrain heard from the artist community when word arrived that the hall was to undergo a major facelift. From the moment Massey Hall welcomed its first audience in 1894, the building's superior acoustics was one element for which the venue was most well-known. The renovation team made sure that all of these newest changes would not negatively affect the acoustics that make Massey a performer's dream venue, but rather that the innovations would enhance the amplified sound to new levels of excellence. This is why Massey Hall brought in Essert.

The first phase of the revitalization began in 2013 with the decommissioning of the obsolete Albert Building (once home to Massey Hall's dressing rooms and offices) and excavation of the expanded footprint directly south of Massey Hall. During this three-year period, construction of the foundation and basement shell for the seven-storey addition was completed and the above-grade structure and slabs were made watertight. Meanwhile, planning and design work for the renovations to the main building continued to move forward, with a 2018 start date scheduled for Phase II.

On July 2, 2018, following three historic performances by Gordon Lightfoot, the hall closed its doors to allow the extensive renovations and construction to proceed. Bringing Massey Hall into the twenty-first century while honouring its history and preserving its legendary acoustics was the top priority of the revitalization team. Grant Troop, vice-president of operations for Massey Hall/Roy Thomson Hall, led this project for the corporation. President and CEO Charlie Cutts hired Troop in 2015 based on the executive's extensive experience managing large capital improvement projects. "This has undoubtedly been the

Grant Troop, vice-president of operations, arrived at Massey Hall in 2015 to lead the revitalization project.

Construction on the upper floors with the Canada Life Building far in the distance.

most interesting part of my career cycle," says Troop. "Just the scope of this project and the national significance of this building … to be involved is truly an honour."

From the outset, Troop made sure all design and building decisions struck a balance between addressing the shortcomings of a 125-year-old building and not changing its essence. "Our number-one priority — and benchmark for success — was to preserve the sanctity of the auditorium," he explains. "We didn't want to mess with anything that would change the intimate connection between audience and artist and make the building feel like it was no longer Massey Hall." To accomplish these lofty goals, Massey Hall worked in close collaboration with dozens of consultants; each expert brought specialized skills and knowledge, but all worked for the project's greater good. Consultants included architects specializing in the restoration of heritage buildings, construction manager EllisDon, acousticians, lighting designers, architectural historians and conservationists, and stained-glass window specialists.

Major highlights of the 2018–21 renovations and revitalization included:

One of the many modern features included in the recent revitalization, retractable seating (for which rails are shown here being installed) allows for general admission access to the floor for select shows.

- replacing the weathered, more-than-seventy-year-old seats on the main floor orchestra and throughout the balcony and adding a *parterre*, a stage-facing seating area around the perimeter of the hall
- installing a deployable seating system that can transform the orchestra level into a standing room (mosh pit!) audience area
- refurbishing the original wood and cast-iron gallery seats with new wood and padded cushions
- restoring the hall's one hundred stained-glass windows, which had been covered since the first half of the century
- returning the Art Deco–style lobby to its previous glory
- completing surface treatments to reinforce the original plaster ceiling, scallops, and rafters
- completing the two-level basement, adding a loading dock, dressing rooms, and technical/production facilities
- refurbishing both the interior and exterior of the hall
- building a seven-storey addition, which included a new stage and expanded basement bar, 500-plus-capacity club, a 150-capacity seated theatre, a recording studio, a lounge, and a cutting-edge performance capture suite
- cleaning and restoring the exterior brick, stone, and metalwork and the hall's iconic neon sign

A glazier at EGD Glass works to restore one of the original century-old stained-glass windows that were boarded up in the early twentieth century to keep out traffic noise and sunlight.

A major upgrade that was undertaken during the two-year revitalization project was the restoration and repair of the original stained-glass windows, which had been covered over since the horse-drawn carriage era. As architectural historian Sharon Vattay (a principal and heritage specialist with GBCA) says, since the original designer, Sidney Rose Badgley, was mainly an architect of churches, it's not surprising he incorporated stained glass in his design.[1] In a 1993 article, "The Hidden Glass Treasures of Massey Hall," York University art historian and Canadian stained-glass expert Shirley Ann Brown explained that some of the windows are art nouveau in style, while a dozen on the main level of the auditorium include life-sized portraits of twelve famous composers — Bach, Beethoven, Mozart, Mendelssohn, Rossini, Chopin, Wagner, Gounod, Schubert, Weber, Handel, and Haydn — surrounded by art nouveau frames and bands. Eight of these survived in place, sandwiched between their protective boards.[2]

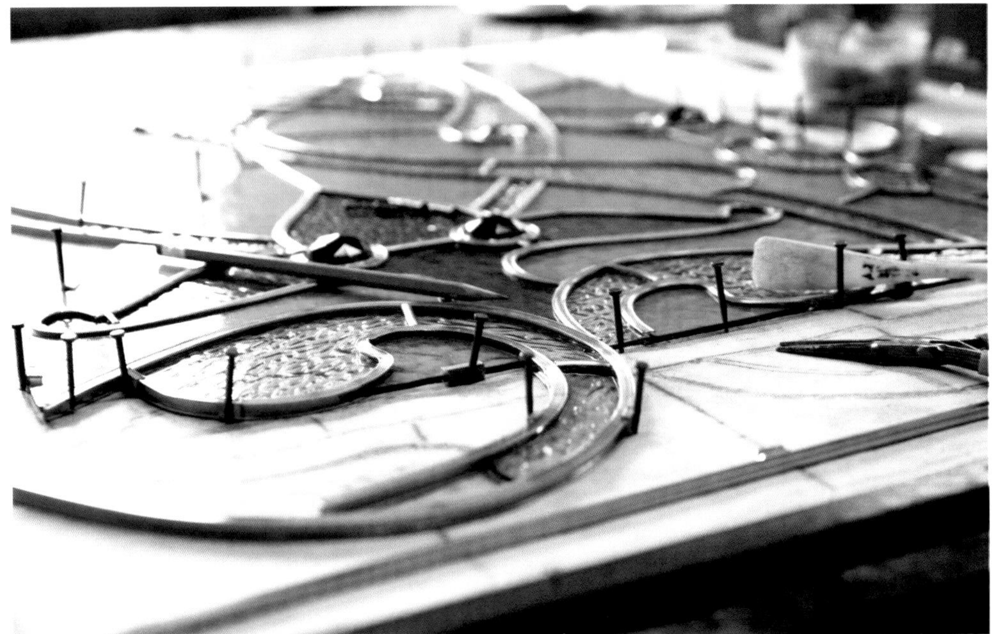

Massey Hall's stained-glass windows were made in the 1890s by Toronto's Faircloth Brothers. As part of the revitalization, these works of art were repaired and restored by EGD Glass and Vitreous Glassworks.

Restoration of the hall's windows, along with other heritage elements such as the intricate plaster arches in the Allan Slaight Auditorium, was made possible by the generous support of government, businesses, leading foundations, and private philanthropists. Experts at Vitreous Glassworks cleaned and repaired these long-forgotten elements of the hall. Heritage approval was granted to remove, label, and crate all one hundred windows in 2017. Each has a number of component sashes (the movable frame of a window that holds the glass) totalling approximately 260 panels. During

> "This revitalization project is as much about bringing Massey Hall into the twenty-first century as it is about preserving its DNA, and ensuring the continued integrity of a valuable space that has been so special for so long."
>
> — Charles Cutts, president and CEO, 1992–2014

"I often tell people that one of the best things about my job is being present for those moments when a whole audience sings together. People are so rarely on the same page; I always feel lucky I get to see that so often. The hall just has this great energy ... it's a music church!"

— Jill Taylor, Massey Hall assistant manager of food and beverage

this removal, the team discovered how neglected they really were. Pigeons had nested between the glass and plywood, and many of the windows were broken and covered with grime. Despite this deterioration, the fact they had been boarded up had also protected them.

The late Deane Cameron, Massey Hall's CEO from 2015 to 2019, said that one day in August 2017, when a number of the windows were being removed, was one of the most emotional moments during the early days of the restoration for him and his staff. "We were all standing there with a lump in our throats," he said.

Eve Guinan and her team of five glazers from the Toronto-based company EGD Glass, who shared the prestigious job of fixing the windows with Vitreous Glass, began the meticulous work of bringing these windows back to life by scrubbing away the dirt, replacing the cracked glass, and touching up any blemishes on the art.

But what about those noise and light issues, the reason the windows were originally boarded up back in the early 1900s? To address these issues, each restored window has now been placed behind a layer of clear glass that protects it from outside elements. Inside, a blackout blind closes off the windows during concerts, while another thick piece of soundproof glass prevents potential noise problems.

Concertgoers want to feel, connect, and escape. As listeners, it's not just about an auditory experience; it's about an *emotional* experience. If you've attended one of the thirty-two shows Blue Rodeo has played at Massey Hall over the past twenty-five years, you've felt the magic of singing along with 2,700 other fans the opening verse and chorus to the 1993 classic "Hasn't Hit Me Yet." Chills occur. This moment is unique to Massey. At other venues, this sing-a-long happens, but not with the same emotional intensity or acoustics. The hall's intimacy and the warmth and clarity of sound reverberating off all surfaces is absorbed by the audience and enhanced by the auditorium's shoebox shape. Its size holds another acoustical advantage; sound strength is greatest in smaller capacity halls since the audience represents the largest absorbing surface.[3]

Artists from all genres — jazz, classical, folk, and rock — have recorded albums at Massey Hall because of its unparalleled sound. Modern high-quality PA systems can present challenges when attempting to produce a successful and appealing sound; yet, with the right equipment and expertise from professional sound engineers, no matter the musical style, superior sound in Massey is usually achieved. Some idiosyncrasies and quirks still existed, but many of these have been addressed by the recent revitalization with the design and installation of a more open array of acoustic surfaces over the stage ceilings to scatter and absorb the echoes. The stage-facing sides of the large arches that span the ceiling have also received a more absorptive surface treatments, as have the wall and ceiling surfaces in the top gallery level.

Massey Hall is regarded as one of the finest sounding concert spaces in the world. Reputations are built note by note, melody by melody, one lyrical line at a time. Each performance builds on this reputation. One acoustic. One voice. No amplification. That's when the grand dame of music halls truly shines.

Acoustician Bob Essert first entered the hall as a patron in the 1980s to see the musical *Cats*. Essert explains the role memories play in a hall's reputation: "Everyone's experience, from artists to patrons, whether they've seen a show live or heard a performance on one of their favourite records recorded at the hall, adds to the venue's mystique and magic and extends those memories." Essert compares Massey Hall to Bristol Beacon (formerly Colston Hall) in Bristol, U.K., which opened in 1867. Both halls were built in a time before sophisticated sound systems; Bristol Beacon also developed a heritage reputation as an exceptional listening venue, hosting many seminal shows, including memorable ones by the Kinks and the Beatles.

Like Bristol Beacon, Massey's acoustics are one of its charms and greatest assets. When the hall was constructed, sound

"People from around the world talk about the sound. It can sound 'boomy,' as it was designed more for acoustic music, but it is spectacular. I notice it. It's pretty special — especially when sound checking and the room is empty — the sound is glorious."

— Gary Craig, drummer (Jann Arden, Anne Murray, Bruce Cockburn, Colin Linden)

> "The quality of the woodwork, the structure, the way the ceiling was designed, the shape of it ... is what makes it stand out [acoustically]."
> — Gordon Lightfoot, singer-songwriter

science, acoustical engineering, and an understanding of the ways architecture and design affect a building's acoustic experience were in their infancy.[4] Yet, when architect Sidney Rose Badgley chose his design — high ceiling, rectangular shape, and horseshoe balconies, the bar for superior sound (while not fully intentional) was set. Right from opening night, the hall's status as an acoustic marvel spread. The *Globe* review of the inaugural concert on June 14, 1894, describes this magic: "Much has been written of the beauty of the hall, its capacity and acoustic properties, but the highest expectations which had been formed from these descriptions were exceeded last night when the hall was seen in all its magnificence of colour and light, filled with an audience of over 4,000 well-dressed people, and when the glorious music of The Messiah was heard with perfect acoustic surroundings."[5]

From this magical beginning more than 127 years ago, Massey's mystique grew with each subsequent performance and each audience member who shared the experience. Besides the artists and audiences, experts in the field of sound studies proclaimed its superiority. For example, professor Fritz Winckel, a German acoustician and musicologist, visited Massey Hall in April 1961 to test its acoustics. Striding to the centre of the stage, he pulled out a .38-calibre revolver and a stopwatch from his coat and fired a loud blank into the galleries. The two-second reverberation time, as well as the hall's dimensions and volume that he had measured, corresponded closely to those of the Grosse Musikvereinssaal in Vienna and the Concertgebouw in Amsterdam. Based on this exercise, Professor Winckel concluded that Massey Hall's acoustics were among the finest in the world.[6]

For others, however, memory and experience elicit less positive feelings about the acoustics of the hall. Some feel the reputation as world-renowned is unwarranted and even exaggerated. One of the main reasons the Toronto Symphony Orchestra (TSO) lobbied for a new venue is that they felt Massey Hall was not well-suited for orchestral music. A TSO musician once said that players could not hear each other clearly because of reverberation, and that consequently a focused ensemble was difficult to achieve.[7] And Edward Pickering, president of the TSO back in 1967 (and

The horseshoe shape of the galleries, so key to the hall's acoustics and sense of intimacy, has been retained.

"When I think about the sound, I think about a Vienna Boys Choir Christmas concert back in the 1970s. I sat in the third level. They didn't use any mics. Just hearing those twenty-five sopranos' and altos' voices ... when the soloist stepped up you could hear every single note he sang up in the third level. That was mind-blowing and magical!"

— Jane Harbury, publicist

> "I started noticing that Massey Hall was another leap for me because it was the first time I could actually hear myself when playing with a band. I could get super quiet and hear it come back like a crystal from the back and thought, this is what music is supposed to be, not struggling to play with a band and get through the songs."[8]
>
> — Jane Siberry, singer-songwriter

later president of Massey Hall), once called the building "appalling for musicians and artists" and described the acoustics as "atrocious."[9]

Despite Pickering's complaints, the prevailing opinion is that Massey Hall is an acoustic gem. The prominent feature of the most successful (and best sounding) halls in the world is their rectangular shape.[10] An identical performance of a piece of music often evokes a stronger emotional impact when presented in the acoustics of a shoebox concert hall. Recent research from Aalto University in Finland reached this conclusion after surveying five of the top halls in the world: Grosse Musikvereinssaal (Vienna), Symphony Hall (Boston), Teatro Colón (Buenos Aires), Konzerthaus (Berlin), and Concertgebouw (Amsterdam). "Some interpretations of the same piece of music can evoke stronger emotions than others. Similarly, our study has succeeded in demonstrating that the hall's acoustics plays an important part in the overall emotional impact. After all, emotional experiences are a key factor in music to many listeners," wrote Dr. Jukka Pätynen.[11]

Massey Hall's shoebox shape significantly impacts the overall acoustics. No matter your seat, the rectangular shape directs how the energies of sound scatter and reverberate throughout the room, so even when sitting in the last seat in the upper balcony, you can hear pre-show chatter on the floor. The acoustics you experience during a show in a sold-out hall are often as warm and clear in these "nose-bleed" seats as if you were sitting front-row centre. This is partly due to the horseshoe shape of the gallery seating, which hugs the audience, adding to the intimacy of the experience. The reverberation from the non-upholstered seating in the upper galleries, especially when the hall is empty, and which many artists experience during sound check, is when sound problems occur. This was Pickering's and the TSO's chief complaint. There is more resonance and an echo occurs.

The "Change Nothing, Improve Everything" edict applied as much to the

Incredible sound and acoustics have been the hallmark of Massey for the past century; that was one of the most sacred pieces that the revitalization project team made sure did not change.

architectural and design enhancements as it did to the ways of improving the natural sound of Massey Hall to better match twenty-first century PA systems. The prevailing goal was to take the hall's sound to a new level of excellence and allow the presentation of a greater variety of events. The mission everyone on the revitalization team followed was to preserve the essential signature — the timbre of the room and tonal quality — but improve the sound for louder amplified concerts by reducing onstage problems for artists. To illustrate, one area the revitalization project addressed is the fact that when the hall is empty, the sound is not the same as when it's full. "The peculiar thing is that Massey Hall always sounded terrible during sound check," says Blue Rodeo's Jim Cuddy. "It was just so *boomy*. There was always a strange bass trap right in the middle. At the beginning you were flipped out by how bad it sounded, but then when the people get in there it sounds absolutely perfect."

Doug McKendrick, vice-president of production for the Corporation of Massey Hall and Roy Thomson Hall, adds: "It's a unique sounding room. Typically, concert halls and rock 'n' roll are at odds with each other. The construction of the balconies and

"It's one of those rooms where, as an artist, it demands you lay it bare. You are close to the audience, so there is no place to hide. Stage left or stage right, the audience is right there. When you hit that sweet spot, there is no place like it. The hall resonates like a beautiful Stradivarius; it has the ability to send that music back out and become part of the instrument and part of the voice."

— Tom Cochrane, singer-songwriter

all the wood in the hall can absorb a lot of bottom end in a way more modern places can't. There is definitely a sweet spot, but if you go above this, it becomes difficult to make it sound good."

This slapback (a doubling echo with a long delay between repetitions of the sound, where individual echoes are perceived) heard on stage is caused by a few of the hall's original architectural features, some of which are heritage elements and cannot be touched, such as the gold arch above the stage. "That's an acoustical liability for amplified sound," Essert explains. "The hard plasters and the curvature of the design reverberates sounds back to the middle of the stage and makes a clap or flutter echo that you can hear thirteen times; it is quite awkward for the performer. It colours the sound blasting out of the stage monitors into the performer's face."

McKendrick explains that everything starts with how loud and clear it sounds on stage. "The stage volume in the monitors is the key. Then, it becomes a fight between the front of house PA and the monitors."

Until 2017, while Massey Hall did have an in-house PA system, including an elaborate fill system designed to address the unique layout and subsequent acoustic challenges it presented, shows typically didn't use it, instead relying on the tour package of the

The upper gallery's wooden seats will be upholstered for better sound absorption and less reverberation when the seats are unoccupied.

incoming performers or a rental system. Every system came in the day of a show and left that day. In some cases, the bookers tried to line up a series of shows that could use common equipment to save on rental costs. This scenario helped make the case for upgrading the house equipment, to alleviate some of these logistical issues and bring more consistency to the sound quality artists hear on stage.

"We wanted a system that virtually no one would refuse," explained McKendrick in an interview with Andrew King for *Professional Sound*. "It is possible to take it down, but we wanted people to walk in and it be a no-brainer that they would use it, so it needed to exceed what people would generally be carrying and provide better coverage than anyone could produce in a one-off scenario."[12]

Massey Hall called in Martin Van Dijk, a senior consultant and partner of Toronto-based audio-visual consultancy firm Engineering Harmonics to help the team

Cross braces hold the newly refurbished windows and their wooden frames in place.

put together specs for the new system. Van Dijk's research included looking at requirements from visiting productions and getting input from a stable of touring audio engineers on their needs and preferences. Besides the main house system, the final proposed solution included a full complement of amplifiers and processing, a replacement of the existing house fills, a small but versatile digital console, and the incorporation of a fibre optic network. Solotech Toronto won the contract in January 2016. The new system was installed in 2017 to rave reviews from touring engineers and bands who plugged into it in the year and a half prior to the closing in July 2018.[13]

One solution to reduce some of the unwanted reverberance in the hall was to design and install a more open array of acoustic surfaces over the stage ceiling to scatter and absorb these echoes, and to fix the plaster in the ceiling. Conserving this heritage aspect of the hall is not just for aesthetics and design, but also to improve the acoustics in the auditorium. "Inside the hall," according to a 2019 article about the project, "the persistently crumbling ceiling is intrinsic to the original Moorish architectural concept and the experience within the space. It will be conserved, but the installation of upgraded acoustical plaster stage-side will enhance the performers' audio feedback."[14]

Another unique sound solution during the revitalization involved the original stained-glass windows being refurbished and put back into place. As mentioned earlier, these will be covered with soundproof glass, and darkened during performances with blackout blinds that can be raised or lowered with the push of a button.

For the audience, new upholstered seating has replaced the old 1948 movie theatre–style reclining seating and the wooden gallery seats, whose acoustic reflectivity had been known to cause headaches. These new upholstered seats will help audio engineers to better span the gulf between mixing in an empty hall at sound check and achieving ideal sound quality when the house fills with people.[15]

# CHAPTER 12

## Artist Development and Outreach

In 2018, following an eight-year journey that began at the Glenn Gould Studio in 2010, Royal Wood made his Massey Hall debut. "I'm grateful and fortunate to say that my headline performance at Massey Hall was a true headline show," says Wood. "I chose to hold out headlining that iconic room until I was able to stand on that stage on my own two feet."[1]

The first show the songwriter ever witnessed at Massey Hall was Lou Reed; it changed his life. "Most musicians have a band in school when they are a kid, and I was no different," Wood recalls. "What made me slightly abnormal though was that my drummer was also my English teacher, Mr. Milner — a dear friend I got to call Andy.

"Knowing my passion for music, my desire to be a professional musician, and my love of the Velvet Underground, Mr. Milner (Andy) decided to take me to Toronto to listen to my hero," he continues. "Thankfully the show was at the

◂ Whitehorse rock Massey Hall on December 8, 2017.

"I think few people realize just how much Massey Hall invests into younger artists to help groom them into becoming Massey Hall ready. I was fortunate enough to be presented by them for years in smaller venues, each time moving up the rung into larger rooms, until I finally made the grade."

— Royal Wood, singer-songwriter

legendary Massey Hall and the moment I walked through its doorway I knew my life had a new mission. I was not only going to make music for a living, I was going to headline Massey one day."

Seeing its grandeur was overwhelming to Wood. Hearing its incredible sound as Lou Reed told him to "take a walk on the wild side" from the stage sent chills. "Sensing the magic every patron felt was infectious," he says. "We were all a part of the fabric of the venue's history. We were all adding more Massey Hall spirits to its story. And somehow we all knew it."

Royal Wood is one of dozens of artists Massey Hall has invested in over the past fifteen years, helping prepare them for the bigger stage — first informally, and then formally, via its strategic Artist Development program. Starting with Whitehorse, and later iskwē, Donovan Woods, Shakura S'Aida, William Prince, and others, this process started organically before evolving into one of the hall's key mandates.

"It's one of those things that is part of our DNA," explains Massey's president and CEO Jesse Kumagai. "We have four charitable objects. One of them is to provide opportunities and to support the development of Canadian talent, but it's not something that had previously been focused on in a meaningful way."

The concept of this Artist Development strategy, which was implemented in the mid-2000s, first as a way to increase the activity in the hall when it was only hosting eighty shows a year, was to help artists on their journey to reach their goal of one day playing Massey Hall. A commissioned report on the economic impact of live music on the City of Toronto, published in the fall of 2020, confirms buildings like Massey Hall play an integral role in an artist's journey: "As part of the music ecosystem, venues are critical for supporting artists' careers, providing the main connection point for audiences to appreciate and discover musicians; and therefore, venues are a cornerstone of artists' career development."[2]

By booking artists at progressively larger spaces, starting at clubs like the Drake Underground and the Rivoli, then building to smaller soft-seaters such as the Glenn Gould Studio, the Winter Garden Theatre, or Harbourfront Centre Theatre, the corporation works with them to grow their audience to the point when, eventually, many of these artists could confidently book a gig at the Shuter Street venue. "We had not worked in external venues before … we just knew we wanted to relate back to those charitable objects and do something more meaningful in terms of artist support," Kumagai explains. "If that meant taking a chance on artists moving up into Massey, this was a good place to start."

> "We believe songwriters like Leif Vollebekk, Shakura S'Aida, William Prince, and Donovan Woods are going to be as important to our future as Gordon Lightfoot, Buddy Guy, or Blue Rodeo have been."
>
> — Stephen McGrath, Massey Hall media and artist development manager

"There are a lot of aspirational venues that artists on their way up want to play," he adds. "Massey Hall is a weird one because it works in both directions: emerging artists dream of playing here, but you also have arena artists who dream of playing Massey; their careers have grown to the point they can headline festivals and play massive venues, but always crave that intimacy of our hall."

He explained that they targeted a handful of Canadian artists they knew already had a solid audience base, drew consistent crowds, and possessed the same quality of the other artists they brought into the hall, but at that point in their careers they needed to make a leap to get up to a room as big as Massey. The corporation started to work with an array of musicians in the Glenn Gould Studio. They identified a pool of artists who

"For me, the beautiful thing about Massey is how it is part of the ecosystem: you need the small venues to get you to Massey. All the other venues I played were stepping stones to get there. It's the barometer. It was like, 'I've played to 3,000 people over six nights at the Horseshoe, can I now put 2,500 in Massey Hall on one night?'"

— Joel Plaskett, musician

had great strengths, knowing not all of them were going to make their way up the venue chain to Massey Hall. "If we did twenty-five artists in the Glenn Gould Studio in one year, the next year five to ten of those might move on to a larger room, and even if just one of them made it to Massey, that was a win for us," Kumagai says.

Whitehorse (Luke Doucet and Melissa McClelland) is an amazing example of one of those "wins" — artists who went from the Glenn Gould Studio to headlining Massey. The first show the corporation promoted with them was booked before the pair had even decided on the name for their new band; it was simply billed as Melissa McClelland and Luke Doucet present Whitehorse.

Luke Doucet grew up in Winnipeg, Manitoba, and quickly discovered Massey Hall's legendary reputation when he started touring the country as a teenager. He first played there as a member of Sarah McLachlan's band and later opened up for Blue Rodeo.

> The story of us getting to Massey was an interesting experience. There was lots of talk about it way before it ever happened. We had meetings with Massey years before we played there, strategizing how we would do it, going from playing a small venue, to a

Whitehorse (Luke Doucet and Melissa McClelland) was one of the first bands that worked with Massey Hall as part of its Artist Development program.

mid-size venue, and then finally playing Massey. I remember rolling my eyes at some of those first meetings, thinking, *You can't predict three years into the future! How can we go from being an unknown band to selling out Massey Hall?* But I was game to try even though I didn't have a whole lot of confidence that it was realistic.

The strategy succeeded. On March 2, 2013, Whitehorse headlined a sold-out show at the hall, touring behind their most recent album, *The Fate of the World Depends on This Kiss*. To mark the occasion, Six Shooter Records released *The Road to Massey Hall*, a six-song EP of the band covering songs of a few of its heroes who had played Massey Hall before them. Songs include Neil Young's "Winterlong," Bob Dylan's "It Ain't Me Babe," and Gordon Lightfoot's "If You Could Read My Mind."

"All the artists we chose to cover songs by not only have played there, but they've all had fairly seminal experiences," Doucet told *The Charlatan*.[3]

When Whitehorse finally booked the monumental gig at Massey, Doucet says he could hear some people laughing at the duo's audacity to think they could fill the hall. "So, we decided on no guest list," he says. "We wanted to prove to ourselves, to our detractors, and to the [music] industry that we had legitimately sold out. My mom flew in from Winnipeg and she even bought a ticket!"

And when the show finally sold out, Doucet admits he was stunned but also humbled. "That show was really heavy in so many ways. I had been there so many times as an opening act or as a hired gun, joining other bands, and there was a bit of that feeling that those appearances didn't count. There were lots of moments just sitting backstage and looking around or pausing while on stage in between songs and looking at the audience and feeling very humble that night to the point of speechlessness."

"Headlining Massey Hall is a lifetime goal and achievement in the career of an artist," says Shauna de Cartier, founder and president of Six Shooter Records. "Eighteen months after launching Whitehorse we accomplished that very thing. In the folk world, this is a meteoric rise."

Before Luke said a word to the crowd or Melissa strummed a chord, the duo received a standing ovation. Jesse Kumagai realized then that they had something going on with the notion of trying to elevate Canadian artists to the next level, especially local artists who had an emotional connection to Massey:

> It was one of the most emotional artist appearances we had ever had in that hall. Just knowing how long they had been striving for that and how important that was to them. You could tell the audience had gone along with these artists for the ride and knew their story. That was a profound moment; it made me realize Canadian artists have a special place in people's hearts at Massey Hall, and the reward for a little bit of effort to make sure those artists could make that leap is huge. That was a real turning point.

Stephen McGrath, Massey Hall's media and artist development manager, who joined the corporation in 2010, says the story of Whitehorse, who have now played Massey Hall multiple times since that sold-out debut in 2013, epitomizes the *raison d'être* of the department he heads, which is a one-person team but is woven into all other areas of the organization. "We are bigger than just bricks," he explains.

> We aspire to be more than just a great-looking building that has beautiful stained-glass windows or where some amazing musical performances happened in the past.

History is happening here every day, and the events occurring now are the stories we'll also be telling well into the future. We believe songwriters like Leif Vollebekk, Shakura S'Aida, William Prince, and Donovan Woods are going to be as important to our future as Gordon Lightfoot, Buddy Guy, or Blue Rodeo have been. These artists will be able to play Massey every year and will have long-standing relationships with their audiences here. Our role is not just about how we help get these artists to Massey Hall, but also how we help them create deeper relationships with audiences once they've arrived.

Since that first Whitehorse show, the hall has worked with countless other Canadian artists in a similar way. Fostering domestic talent and investing in their careers is now an integral part of the hall's strategic plan. By using its ability and resources, they spot talented artists who are in a position of growth, regardless of their label affiliation or financial situation, and whom they believe have the best opportunity to succeed. Massey Hall has not only become a key partner in the growth of artists' careers, but also a trusted curator for the introduction of new sounds to audiences from Toronto and beyond.

"I've made it my own career goal to promote a hundred shows at this iconic venue. With the support of the visionary people behind the scenes at Massey Hall, I may very well achieve this grand master plan. Their boundless passion for and commitment to artist development embodies the spirit and energy of the hallowed hall they serve."

— Shauna de Cartier, founder and president, Six Shooter Records

Other ways the corporation helps grow Canadian talent include supporting studio and live recordings, creating press kits and artist biographies, facilitating photo shoots, providing media training and strategic planning workshops, and creating promotional videos, podcasts, short films, live sessions, music videos, and thirty-minute concert films.[4] It's about giving these artists the tools and resources they need to reach the next level in their careers. It's not a cookie-cutter approach. What an artist like William Prince requires and what will work for them differs from what works for an artist like Shakura S'Aida. "We are there to support each artist individually," explains McGrath.

New Brunswick bluesman Matt Andersen at Massey in March 2014 for his headline debut.

"We work with them and their teams as a strategic partner … we are just one spoke on that wheel, to help them not just grow, but to also sustain, their audience. We are behind them for the long term. It's not just about the next show or the next album cycle. We want to make artists feel like they belong here. If they need resources, we are here to support them."

In 2010, Massey Hall started working with East Coast bluesman Matt Andersen, and by 2014, more than seven thousand people had seen the songwriter perform in a variety of Toronto venues.[5] Andersen made his headline debut at Massey on March 1, 2014, shortly after the release of his tenth album, *Weightless*; he reached that stage on his own merits, thanks in part to Massey Hall's nurturing. Previously, the corporation had presented him at the Glenn Gould Studio and the Winter Garden; he was also a special guest opening a Buddy Guy Massey Hall show in 2011. Through this partnership, the corporation worked collaboratively with Andersen and his team to help cultivate his relationship with current — and future — fans. This strategy included releasing a special online video to media before his headline gig, featuring him on the cover of the season's brochure, and showcasing the artist performing solo acoustically at Massey Hall, filling the venue with his impressive voice and passionate guitar playing.[6]

"My folks flew in for the show," recalls Andersen. "People watching me for many years got excited. I had started playing at clubs for two or three people. I consider myself fortunate to just do it once."

Growing up in New Brunswick, Andersen learned about Massey Hall by watching MuchMusic, as the VJs often talked about all the bands currently on tour and Massey was the place many went when in Toronto. "Massey Hall in Canada holds a lot of weight," Andersen says. "I felt that weight and reverence. Seeing your name on the marquee there is a dream. I don't get

East Coast rocker Matt Mays aspired to headline Massey Hall for years. On May 4, 2018, his dream came true; he rose to the occasion and his fans embraced him.

nervous before a lot of gigs, but that one I did … just the size of the room. All my management was there. The place was full. I showered before the gig and walked out on stage with my zipper still down; that broke the ice! You can't get much worse than that."

Fellow East-Coaster Matt Mays aspired for years to one day play Massey Hall. His first time on the stage was May 16, 2006, when his band, Matt Mays and El Torpedo, opened for the Black Crowes on their cross-Canada tour, but the dream fully materialized when he headlined there on May 4, 2018, just a couple of months before the venue closed for renovations. "I always wanted to play Massey," Mays recalls. "I mowed lawns a whole summer to buy my first decent electric guitar at Steve's Music [in Toronto] and that same day I walked by Massey Hall and discovered its lore."

Mays believes the place is so regal that when the call came, and the reality set in that he was going to headline the hall with his band, he knew he needed to rise to the occasion. "The venue demands that of you, but that helps to get rid of the nerves," he explains. "I received a warm hug from the ghosts of the place; they extract the nerves from you and all you have left is this freight train of magic that you hop onto and everything else flows from there. You can then let go of the wheel and just let the show happen."

That's exactly what Mays did. The show was recorded for a *Live at Massey Hall* series, and friends, fellow artists, and long-time fans — which included actor Eugene Levy and his family — were there to cheer him and his bandmates on. And, while the artist normally doesn't enjoy listening to his shows since it might ruin his impression of how the gig went, this is one time he got the nerve up to listen to the tapes. "I listened and could hear my band and the ghosts really took over. I play with those guys every night and it was beautiful listening to them in my headphones. It confirmed that it really happened, it wasn't a myth, or not just in my head. That's pretty cool. I feel good about nicking my tiny notch of music history into that place."

Peter Katz is another artist who hopes to one day fulfill his dream of standing on that stage, performing to a sold-out audience as Mays did. The JUNO nominee and CBC Galaxie Rising Star Award winner first got involved with Massey Hall in 2013 when they promoted him in a double-bill at the Rivoli with fellow Canadian singer-songwriter Emma-Lee. "I had seen what they'd done for artists like Whitehorse, building them up from venue to venue, and was really keen to be on that path," Katz recalls. The songwriter struck up a conversation with Stephen McGrath. The pair felt a connection and stayed in touch. It wasn't long until Massey Hall formally took the artist under its wing and began to collaborate on a long-term strategy to grow his audience. The next step on the road to Massey was an album-release show in 2015 for *We Are the Reckoning* at Harbourfront Centre. The show sold out well in advance, proving the momentum was building. "After that show, Stephen and I shared a meal together and conjured up the vision of headlining Massey Hall one day," Katz explains. "We started working backwards from there. Stephen has been deeply involved in my career ever since. I'm talking hundreds, if

"I felt like I was in a dream, standing on the same wood as my heroes. My shoes touching the memory of their shoes. Up there, time disappears, history is brought into the present and the present is made historic."

– Serena Ryder, JUNO award–winning songwriter

not thousands of hours [spent] working on supporting my new album *City of Our Lives*, which was released in 2020."

"From encouraging me to stretch my writing, to listening to over sixty new songs and selecting the tracks for the album, to connecting me with producers, to conceiving of the live show, to being on the other end of the phone when I was in the hospital, and everything in between," Katz adds. "I feel a deep sense of gratitude to [Stephen] and the whole team. I feel like I'm walking into my family house when I walk through the offices there. I feel like I worked my whole career to have a team like this supporting me; it put a lot of wind in my sails."

Canadian blues vocalist, songwriter, and actress Shakura S'Aida describes the Massey program as a "life-changer" for her. "I'd travelled on tour, taking my music to thirty countries, and yet, before I became a part of Massey Hall's Artist Development program, I really didn't know how to bring myself to another level, so I could be self-sufficient as an artist. It's so hard for a lot of people in my community to just reach that next level."

Massey Hall's support allowed S'Aida to stretch her art to levels and places she didn't imagine possible. It has also opened new doors for her. When talking about this unwavering support, the songwriter gets emotional. "When they told me in a meeting once, 'We believe in you. We have your back!' I broke down," she recalls. "I can tell you in my thirty-year career I have had very few people say this to me. When their team said this … it changed my entire

Toronto blues artist Shakura S'Aida always thrills — and brings chills to audiences — with her powerful pipes.

outlook. I went through Covid-19 without panic. I'm not scared anymore because I've learned the new skills to help me get through and make me stronger as an artist. As a Black woman in this industry, it's the difference between playing in juke joints or having my mom still manage me to me doing it with an amazing team of people who believe in me."

As another way to raise the profile of and support Canadian artists like Katz, the corporation launched a new program during the 2013/14 season. The *Live at Massey Hall* concert film series (liveatmasseyhall.com) involved filming thirty-minute concert videos and interviews that captured a variety of domestic artists the hall was currently nurturing. Bands in that first year included Timber Timbre, Cœur de pirate, Great Lake Swimmers, Cold Specks (who now performs as Ladan), and Basia Bulat. Unlike the other artists who had headlined Massey, these were bands in a variety of genres that had a sizable enough audience base to fill the hall but whose fans were not ready to drop big dollars on tickets. Kumagai explains:

> We're a charitable not-for-profit and through the support of donors and funding bodies, we were able to make these concerts more accessible, offering lower ticket prices, many at $18.94 as a nod to the year the hall opened. With many of these artists performing at Massey Hall for the first time, we filmed the concerts so we could share the footage with a global audience and showcasc amazing contemporary Canadian artists in the magic of Massey Hall.

Before he ever stood on Massey's stage, Shad's first experience with the venue was a Sigur Rós show in 2005. "I distinctly remember thinking that I could never fill this place," he recalls. Next thing you know, the rapper stepped onto the stage in 2013, opening for Maestro Fresh Wes, when the godfather of Canadian hip-hop performed his groundbreaking *Symphony in Effect* album in celebration of the record's twenty-fifth anniversary. Shad made his headlining debut March 27, 2015, thanks to the support of the corporation's Artist Development program. The electrifying performance by the JUNO award–winning rapper was captured on film as part of season two of the *Live at Massey Hall* series. "The whole series does a great job of honouring Canadian musicians and the fans who have made the culture of live music in this country so great," Shad says.

Headlining Massey Hall was a special moment in Shad's career, not just for him, but also for his fans. "I recognized so many faces — either family or friends or fans that have seen me many times. It was special for them to get to see me in this nice room after so many little sweaty shows! It was like old friends, who are used to hanging out at each other's houses, deciding to get dressed up and go do something different." He also pointed out that after working at his craft for more than ten years and releasing four albums "it felt like the culmination of something ... like we were all kind of enjoying our shared history." He was worried a bit about the seating at Massey. "My shows don't really work unless people are on their feet — but everyone was up for the whole show. It was just the perfect night."

Japandroids is another band that has benefitted from the ongoing *Live at Massey Hall* concert and film series. On October 24, 2017, the Vancouver alternative-rock duo Brian King and David Prowse, like so many of their musical heroes before them, headlined the Massey stage. The gig was more than just another stop on their exhaustive *Near to the Wild Heart of Life* global tour to promote the record of the same name — a tour that saw the pair play 150 shows in twenty-three countries between October 2016 and October 2018. Were they nervous? Definitely. Excited? Damn right. "There is no other venue it compares to," says drummer/vocalist Prowse. "It is the

Canadian hip-hop star and JUNO-award winner Shad credits the Artist Development program for his success. He played to a sold-out crowd on March 27, 2015.

Canadian indie rockers Japandroids are part of Massey's Artist Development program. They headlined the venue in October 2017, recorded it as part of the *Live at Massey Hall* series, and released a record, *Massey Fucking Hall*, in 2020.

stage to play as far as storied and historic rooms." Prowse admits he had mixed feelings heading into this show. For one, a soft-seater like Massey Hall is not a typical locale to see a Japandroids show. "The opportunity was presented to us and we couldn't really say no," Prowse explains. "There was a brief moment of hesitation where we wondered whether it was the right move for us at the time and the right space to play, then we just said 'Fuck it!'" Walking onstage to an empty auditorium for sound check that October afternoon, the gravitas of the moment really materialized for him.

"That's when it really hit me," he recalls. "The sense of history there is so palpable. I don't get that very often from other venues. Just looking out at the plush seats and the multiple balconies, you feel so small and the room is so gigantic." While every Japandroids show feels cathartic, nothing could top the emotional energy and release he felt that night. "There were a couple of moments while we were playing, I got kind of misty," he recalls. "I had a moment of reflection where I paused and just thought, *Holy shit! Look how far we've come.* I'm so grateful I had that moment."

On June 26, 2020, Japandroids released *Massey Fucking Hall.* The twelve-track album documents this milestone. Some songs in their setlist from that night didn't make the record, especially one special cover, apropos for the venue — the band's take on the Tragically Hip's "Nautical Disaster." Gord Downie had died only a week before, and his loss still hung heavy in the hearts and conscience of the nation. As a band, the Hip was a touchstone for both Prowse and King as they forged their own path on the indie-rock highway. It was a fitting tribute in a venue Gord revered. "Playing that song at that moment in time at that venue was the emotional peak for me," Prowse says.

• • •

Over the years, a diverse range of performers in every genre imaginable have participated in Massey Hall's Artist Development programs. One of these artists is iskwē. Born in Winnipeg, the Cree/Dene singer-songwriter now resides in Montreal. She first stepped onto Massey's stage as part of the lineup for a bill called AGO Creative Minds at Massey Hall. In this celebration of the arts, the JUNO-nominated songwriter joined writer Salman Rushdie, performance artist Andrea Fraser, and filmmaker Charles Officer. Later, in 2019 and 2020, she played a pair of sold-out shows at the Mod Club, which were presented by Massey Hall. "They are not afraid of supporting and being a part of tough conversations," iskwē says. "They get their hands dirty, have chats and always think of ways they can be better as an institution when it comes to Indigenous artists."

What iskwē admires the most about her relationship with the corporation is that it doesn't feel like a business transaction. That is what stands out for her and makes the relationship extra meaningful. "They support and encourage my project ideas and take time to sit with me and brainstorm," she says. "It's beyond them just putting money and resources behind the artist and hoping for the best. They invest time, energy, and offer creative suggestions."

iskwē took to the stage at Roy Thomson Hall as a special guest in the annual Dream Serenade benefit concert in 2018.

• • •

Education and community outreach have been a growing focus at the corporation over the last few years. This community focus links to the corporation's core mission and mingles with its Artist Development strategy. These innovative programs centre on the power of music to connect, inspire, transform, and enrich audiences. Their programs take place in the halls, in schools, and in the community. Artists and audiences are brought together through concerts, music-making, and interactive experiences, creating connections with diverse communities, from new Canadians to new mothers.

Prior to 2017, the long-running program *Share the Music* stood alone in bringing music to young people across the Greater Toronto Area. Since 2017, when a full-time manager was hired to fulfill this mandate, and the not-for-profit received a sizable donation from a Canadian private holding company, they've expanded their programming and developed further resources for schools, youth, and other community members. Vanessa Smith, the education and outreach manager, started by completing research about what other comparable halls were doing with respect to education and outreach. Then she surveyed patrons and donors to understand what about the hall really resonated with them. She also interviewed teachers to learn what types of extracurricular activities they felt would supplement the work they were doing in the classroom. With all of this research, Smith and her team worked with teaching artists and community partners to create several new programs.

*Share the Music* began in 1999 and enables local youth of all backgrounds to attend mainstage performances and pre-show workshops, with complimentary tickets distributed to schools and community groups. Since its inception, the program has provided free tickets to more than twenty-two thousand guests (ages eight to eighteen) for 129 events and counting. The program has enabled youth from over 150 schools and 100 different community groups to visit both venues to experience a diverse range of programming that includes classical, jazz, blues, chorale, pop, and spoken word performances. Many of the events have focused on music from around the world. In addition to the concerts, two or three artist educators take the program directly to the schools each year. "Growing up, music was not only my passion, but it was my saviour," says Royal Wood, who worked with Massey Hall on a program called *Collaborations*. "It marked all the moments in my life — both good and bad. When Massey Hall asked me to speak to children about music and the importance of it in our life, not to mention write a song with them, I jumped at the chance. You never know when, and where, you can make a difference and steer a child down a better path."

Through assembly-style presentations and smaller workshops, artists visit students in grades four through twelve to discuss music, songwriting, civic engagement, and facing your fears. Since the *Share the Music* program began, Massey Hall has expanded its education and outreach offerings to students through a variety of new programs. Besides Royal Wood, visiting artists who have participated in these educational initiatives have included Liz Lokre, Peter Katz, and the Good Lovelies. Katherine Fraser, a teacher with the Toronto District School Board, was working at Indian Road Crescent Junior Public School when Royal Wood visited their school as part of the *Collaborations* project to work with her students on creating a song. "Our students were very excited to have a pop star come to our music room," says Fraser, who is also a professional musician. "It was a group effort to communicate and create with my students. Many educators helped and the students worked tirelessly to improve their song. They were really inspired by Royal Wood's musicianship." As part of this program, Indian Road Crescent Junior Public School students attended Royal's Massey Hall headlining debut, hung out backstage, and watched the artist — from sound check to the encore. "Some day they may follow in Royal Wood's footsteps but I bet they will remember the experience and dream up their own path," Fraser adds.

Teaching artist Peter Katz (centre) meets Shakaila and her daughter backstage at Massey Hall in May 2018.

Royal Wood collaborates with a class of students at Indian Road Crescent Junior Public School as part of one of Massey Hall's education and outreach programs.

In the 2006/07 academic year, the Ontario Ministry of Education created the Specialized High Skills Major (SHSM) program to give high school students the opportunity to focus on a particular career field and receive specialized instruction from professionals in that field. Massey Hall's SHSM workshops provide opportunities for Arts and Culture and Non-Profit SHSM students to explore the business of music and entertainment through workshops in performance, songwriting, event management, publicity, digital music manipulation, video game music, and more.

Sound Museum is another meaningful project that takes Massey Hall to local schools and the world via an online Creative Commons repository of sounds. A team of sound engineers, percussionists, and educators walked through the historic venue prior to its temporary closure and revitalization, and captured recordings as they went. Sounds captured include everything from a ticket being ripped to a coin rolling across the stage. A teacher resource guide with suggested apps and activities helps teachers use the sounds in a classroom setting.

Teaching artist Liz Lokre, participant Lexie and her daughter, and musician Adrian X perform Lexie's lullaby "I Got You" at a Lullaby Project concert in 2019.

Focusing on the power of music to enrich lives, Massey Hall's community engagement activities are created in partnership with others who share this vision, and strive to be accessible, inclusive, and, above all, innovative. The following two programs focus on music's ability to empower, inspire, connect, and transform.

The LETS (Learn English Through Song) program uses a mix of popular music and songs written specifically for ESL instruction. A music teacher works in tandem with community partners such as NEW (Newcomer Women's Services Toronto) to teach vocabulary, idioms, and everyday expressions through music in these ten-week programs. For example, they used Royal Wood's "A Good Enough Day" as part of their online work during the pandemic to talk about the sun and light as a metaphor for happiness and to focus on the good. This allowed the organizers to bring light and hope to the participants at a most difficult time.

The Lullaby Project pairs parents with Canadian songwriters to create, record, and perform a lullaby for their child. Often these lullabies pull away from the traditional lullaby format and become complex creations that express the challenging experience of parenthood and the parent's hopes and dreams for the child. The program originated at the Weill Music Institute at Carnegie Hall,

Baby Lorenzo gets familiar with the mixing board at Toronto studio Revolution Recording as part of the Lullaby Project.

and the Corporation of Massey Hall and Roy Thomson Hall became a Lullaby Project partner in 2017. The halls partner with Jessie's: The June Callwood Centre for Young Women,[7] writing lullabies with mothers and mothers-to-be aged fourteen to twenty-one.

Peter Katz is just one Canadian songwriter who has participated in the Lullaby Project. In his career, there are few experiences he has had that have been this powerful and uplifting. He recalls the day he met the young mother he had been paired with and how special the experiences was. "I got to meet Shakaila for the first time at Jessie's Centre. We clicked right away. She told me about how she called her daughter 'Mya Papaya' and immediately I had that little melody in my head. I wanted it to really feel like it was from her … we worked together to craft lyrics that were really in her voice. It was such a beautiful experience. And then of course, getting to record it together, and hearing her read the dedication to Mya that plays at the top of the song … I don't think you can be a human with a heart and not be moved by that!"

When Shakaila first learned about the opportunity to participate in the Lullaby Project, she was excited, but also very nervous. She thought, "I don't know how to write a song … I can't sing!" After she met Peter, her nerves settled, especially when she learned he had worked with American singer-songwriter Ingrid Michaelson's producer, an artist the new mom admired. "It was a perfect match," says Shakaila. "The songwriting process was way easier than I imagined … the love I have for my daughter just poured out onto the page and we made it into a beautiful and very catchy song." Three years since the pair collaborated on "Oh My Mya,"

Shakaila still sings it with Mya every night before bed, or whenever her daughter is overwhelmed. The Lullaby Project is the program Vanessa Smith is the proudest of:

> You would think the result would be a simplistic melody, but the moms often bond with these songwriters and write vulnerable, raw pieces about teen motherhood and some of the difficulties that entails. It's a really neat project, not just about bonding, but mothers can then take these songs and sing them to their babies for the rest of their lives.

Other community outreach programs that have been launched at Massey include Call & Response, a volunteer program for Toronto-area secondary school students that consists of ten weeks of skill development through the lens of various art forms — discussing communication in a beatboxing workshop, teamwork through improvisation, self-esteem through songwriting, finding your voice through opera singing, and more. Participants are also required to sign up for volunteer shifts to assist in education and outreach programming, helping them to earn the community-service hours required for the Ontario Secondary School Diploma. During the Covid-19 pandemic, Shakura S'Aida participated in this educational program, delivering a couple of virtual workshops to high school students. "I spoke to them about protest music and songwriting," she says. "I even had my mom come on the Zoom call to share her experiences of participating in the Civil Rights movement in the 1960s, protesting inequalities and getting arrested. The program is amazing. Watching them sit in those Zoom rooms and create these protest songs and write music with a message gave me hope for the next generation."

All these educational programs are to continue when the revitalized Massey Hall opens. New programs will also be added as the corporation strengthens its focus on music education, community outreach, and artist development. Jesse Kumagai says that "everything we have done to date has been a pilot project." They are ready to roll out all of these programs in an even more meaningful way in the revitalized hall with its new performance spaces and additional amenities, such as a broadcast studio. "Those are all a huge part of our future and the magic formula of programming mixed with brick-and-mortar that will dovetail together," he adds.

MASSEY MUSIC HALL

# CHAPTER 13

# Legendary Leaders

For any organization to not just survive but thrive for more than a century, great leadership is required. From the time Massey Hall opened its doors, there have been many exceptional individuals who are as important to the hall as the bricks and mortar on which its foundation is built. From Sir Ernest MacMillan, who led the TSO for a quarter century, to the late Deane Cameron, who spearheaded the revitalization of Massey Hall, serving as president and CEO from September 2015 until he passed away in 2019, five legendary leaders are remembered for their passion, impact, and legacy.

## Sir Ernest MacMillan: Conductor of Massey's Hall's "Golden Age"

Born in Mimico, Ontario, the year before Massey Hall opened, Ernest MacMillan began composing music at an early age. His first Massey Hall experience came

◂ With the fire escapes removed and the bricks cleaned and repaired during the revitalization, the hall's original name etched into the facade is visible once again.

in April 1904, when the ten-year-old piano prodigy played the organ for the Methodist Social Union's Festival of the Lilies. The press lauded his debut: "It seemed almost eerie to see the youngster commanding so much music, this lad in a white sailor suit, whose feet could barely reach the pedals."[1]

In 1931, MacMillan was hired as the conductor of the TSO, succeeding Luigi von Kunits, and ended up serving the longest tenure as conductor in the symphony's history. In *Intimate Grandeur*, William Kilbourn writes of MacMillan's seminal time at the helm: "The quarter century from 1931 to 1956, before television had become the dominant form of mass culture, can fairly be described as Massey Hall's Golden Age. It is not altogether a coincidence that this very same quarter century included the twenty-five seasons in which the most versatile musical genius in Canadian history was at the helm of the Toronto Symphony Orchestra."[2]

The Canadian Trio (Zara Nelsova, Sir Ernest MacMillan, Kathleen Parlow), during the early 1940s.

In his first season as TSO conductor, MacMillan introduced full-length evening concerts. In his second season (1932/33), he moved all shows to Tuesday nights at eight-thirty and raised ticket prices from seventy-five cents to $2.50, though some select seats were kept at fifty cents.[3] In 1935, MacMillan became the only Canadian musician ever recognized with a knighthood. Writes Kilbourn, "Sir Ernest knew how to use his skills on the podium to cast a spell upon his audience and induce them to share his total attention to even the most difficult of the great music he loved. No magician ever made better use of his wand or his arms, or for that matter the language of his whole body."[4]

Later, MacMillan conducted choral music with a conservatory choir from Convocation Hall, which moved into Massey Hall, giving concerts with and without the TSO. After the Mendelssohn Choir fell on hard times in 1940 and had to cancel its season, it eventually led to the two choirs being merged under MacMillan; he led the new Mendelssohn Choir for fourteen years.[5] Beginning in 1944, the Mendelssohn Choir performed *The Messiah* every Christmas at Massey Hall. In 1956, MacMillan retired as conductor of both the TSO and the Mendelssohn Choir, and in 1969 he was named a Companion of the Order of Canada. Sir Ernest MacMillan died in May 1973. Reflecting back on his impact twenty-six years later, the *Ottawa Citizen*, honouring his legacy, wrote, "Canadians mourned the passing of the man who had ushered in the country's musical coming of age."[6]

### Joe Cartan: From Usher to General Manager, Fifty-Five Years in the Hall

Few people in the history of Massey Hall spent as much time within its four walls and knew the building as intimately as Joe Cartan. He started as an usher in 1929, rose to head usher by 1940, joined the permanent staff as assistant manager in 1945, and from 1968 until his retirement in 1984 he was the hall's general manager. Most nights, while patrons enjoyed the performances, Cartan was busy in his office tallying up box office receipts.[7] He usually arrived by ten in the morning and left following the evening's concert around eleven o'clock.[8]

In an interview with the *Globe and Mail* in 1981, Cartan recalled how he landed his first job at Massey Hall when he was only fourteen years old. The assistant manager, Jack Carter, was a friend of his father's. The starting pay was fifty cents a night and Cartan turned up to his first shift wearing

A historic program from 1894, the year Massey Hall opened.

A collage of past posters in Centuries bar pays homage to some of the incredible jazz shows that Massey Hall has presented over its 127-year history.

knickerbockers. Afterward, Carter told Cartan's dad, "If this kid's going to come and usher down here, you'd better get him a long pair of pants."

Cartan also recalled the boxing and wrestling matches that were held at Massey Hall:

> In the late thirties there was a man named Deacon Allen. His advertisements read, "The best fights of all go at Massey Hall." He had all the fighters on stage: Little Arthur King, Tommy Bland, Baby Yak. About the same time, Ivan Mickailoff ran wrestling [there]. Ivan was often in the ring three times a night when headliners didn't show. He'd fight men like the head-butting Gus the Goat, Count Zarinoff, and Danno O'Mahoney, who held his opponents in the air like the Statue of Liberty holds her torch. Sometimes the entire ring would collapse and the audience would have to wait while a stage crew reassembled it.

### John Lawson: The Lawson Legacy

Born in Toronto just thirty-two years after Massey Hall opened its doors, John Lawson's ties to the venue span more than a generation. For many years, his father, Hugh H. Lawson, was chair of Massey Hall. John Lawson practised commercial and corporate law in Toronto as a partner with McCarthy Tétrault Barristers & Solicitors for more than forty-four years. When he was not practising law, Lawson was giving back to his community. Following in his father's footsteps, he became a member of the Board of Trustees of Massey Hall in 1972 while he was president of the Toronto Mendelssohn Choir (TMC) and also a director of the Toronto Symphony Orchestra. In the early 1970s, the Board of Trustees was expanded to prepare for the construction of a new concert hall. As a board member, Lawson was active in the hall's daily affairs. Later, when Edward Pickering, the first president of Roy Thomson Hall, retired in 1988, Lawson succeeded him as (volunteer) president and took early retirement from his law firm. The president was not only the chief executive officer but also the chief operating officer, and in this capacity he ran both concert halls more or less on a full-time basis until 1992 when the corporation appointed its first full-time professional president (Charles Cutts). Lawson also served as chair of the Board during this period, retiring from that position in 1993.

### Charles Cutts: "Improve Everything, Change Nothing" — Preserving the Spirit of the Hallowed Hall

From sitting in the balcony as a patron watching Bob Dylan get booed when he went electric with the Hawks back in 1965 to leading Massey Hall as its president and CEO for twenty-two years (1992–2014), Charles Cutts is another of the hall's legendary leaders.

Cutts began his career in 1969 as a chartered accountant. He also served as general manager of the O'Keefe Centre (now Meridian Hall) before taking the helm of

> "First time I played [the hall], with Great Lake Swimmers, was amazing … such a cool room. It feels so big and yet so cozy.… That's what coaxes out all these great performances."
>
> — Miranda Mulholland, fiddler, singer, and vice chair of the Massey board

Charles Cutts served as president and CEO of Massey Hall and Roy Thomson Hall from 1992 until his retirement in 2014.

Massey Hall and Roy Thomson Hall in 1992. The seeds for the current revitalization were planted during the final years of Cutts's tenure. In announcing the $135-million project in February 2015, Cutts said, "Massey Hall is not only a national historic site that we all treasure, but a place where Canadian music history is made. It's been that way for the last 120 years, and will be for the next 120."[9]

Later, in an interview with journalist Juliette Jagger, he added, "Something that dates as far back as Hart Massey himself who, being a frugal businessman, was simply never able to strike a deal for it. Now, there has been a meeting of the minds and we finally have the opportunity to improve upon, enhance, and revitalize the Massey Hall we have all come to know and love."[10]

Cutts further explained the vision of the multiphase revitalization project:

> One of the magic phrases we have been using to describe the revitalization project is "improve everything, change nothing." Massey Hall is all about the interior audience chamber. Now, that doesn't sound glamorous, but there is a fundamental spatial relationship that exists between the artist and the audience within that room and that is incredibly special. There's just something about the way the space is configured that has stood the test of time. An artist can stand at centre stage and feel as though they can touch every single person in the room and the audience will always be close enough to see the sweat on the performer's brow. That experience, that

closeness, that's what gives Massey Hall such magic, and that is as relevant today as it was in the past and will continue to be down the line.[11]

## Deane Cameron: Captain Canada's Legacy

A passionate leader and a mentor to many in the music industry, Deane Cameron sadly passed away on May 16, 2019, before seeing his vision for a revitalized Massey Hall completed. His death was a huge loss for the Canadian music industry. Even before he arrived at Massey Hall as president and CEO in September 2015, he had left a legacy. Cameron, known as Captain Canada to many for the way he always championed Canadian and Indigenous artists, was the head of Capitol Records-EMI Music Canada for twenty-five years. The honours he received were countless — from a Walt Grealis Special Achievement Award JUNO to the Order of Canada.

Cameron's commitment to the revitalization and renewal of Massey Hall is now forever stamped on the building. His spirit joins the visionary leaders who came before him. "Because we are a not-for-profit organization, every motivation, every move we make is to do the right thing at the right time for the right artist," Cameron explained.

The late Deane Cameron (president and CEO of Massey Hall from 2015 to 2019) poses with Jim Cuddy on Massey Hall Day (June 14, 2018) following a concert to celebrate the hall's 124th birthday.

Long before taking the helm at the hall, Cameron was familiar with Massey's magic. The first show he saw there was the Band in 1970, when he sat in the balcony with school chum Tom Cochrane. The pair played together in a band called Harvest: Deane was the drummer and Tom the singer and guitarist. "We were such fanatics of the Band, we bought the tickets the minute they went on sale. I'll never forget the feeling Tom and I had of finally seeing Robbie Robertson up close. After I saw Levon Helm play, that was the beginning of my decline and giving up on being a drummer. He was so amazing. It made me think, *I will never be able to get anywhere near that level of excellence and also sing*."

Cameron's love for the hall started then. "It gave me the feeling I was somewhere special."

Before Cameron arrived in 2015, the revitalization of Massey Hall was already underway. "It was an honour when I was approached to come here," he said. "It feels like the final couple of years of a high school/university degree."

From 2015 until his death in 2019, Cameron carried on the work begun by his predecessor, always keeping the hall's rich legacy in the forefront in all decisions. "The motivation here, started by … Charlie Cutts, is that we always wanted to expand somehow and in some way at Massey Hall, but we just didn't have the space, other than the Albert Building eking out a few more dressing rooms," Cameron said. "Charlie wanted to do it, but never had any land available. When the opportunity came up to have land deeded to us through MOD Tricon in a section 37 exchange for their condo facing Yonge Street, the team took that, realized it was now or never, grabbed it, and ran with it."

Cameron described the revitalization as transformational. "It is going to give us so much more to do when it comes to artist development and education and in outreach because we will simply have space to do these things."

Cameron's death in 2019 sent shockwaves throughout the music industry. Not just because of the hole he left at the helm of Massey Hall but also for the loss to his extended family, which included artists, managers, and anyone touched by his passion and jovial disposition. These were big shoes to fill. Fortunately, ready and willing was Jesse Kumagai — a leader who first joined the organization in 2003 and whom Cameron wooed back to Massey Hall in 2016. After an external international search, the Board of Governors of the Corporation of Massey Hall and Roy Thomson Hall named the Torontonian to the position of president and CEO, effective February 26, 2020, succeeding interim leader Thomas C. MacMillan.

Kumagai has brought the same passion as Cameron to the position. "These halls and the incredible people who pour their hearts into every show have become like family to me," he said following this announcement. "I can't imagine a greater honour than to be

The long-forgotten stained-glass windows restored and back where they belong.

trusted with the responsibility of leading this profoundly talented team into the most exciting period in our history."

Reflecting on Cameron's legacy, Kumagai says his predecessor brought a fresh perspective to the organization and a unique appreciation for the artists, which he had gained during his time as the president of EMI Canada. "It was Deane's passion for identifying, nurturing, and promoting emerging artists that really helped boost our Artist Development program and give it momentum. The power of music education is something else that was near and dear to Deane's heart and he was always a champion for Indigenous artists … that's one more piece of his legacy."

# CHAPTER 14

## A Beacon of Hope

On Sunday, June 6, 2021, during the fiftieth JUNO Awards telecast, the public got its first glimpse of the inside of the revitalized hall. Perched in the upper gallery, Geddy Lee and Alex Lifeson of Rush presented the Tragically Hip with the Humanitarian Award, an annual honour that recognizes an outstanding Canadian artist or music industry leader for their commitment to social, environmental, or humanitarian causes. Then Gordon Lightfoot introduced the band, who performed live on TV for the first time since frontman Gord Downie's death in 2017. Leslie Feist joined Hip members Rob Baker, Gord Sinclair, Johnny Fay, and Paul Langlois and sang "It's a Good Life If You Don't Weaken."

A harbinger of hope, this emotional performance signalled that the return of live music to the hall was imminent. Two weeks later, when Massey Hall turned 127 years old (June 21, 2021), the corporation announced its planned reopening. Tagged "Let's Meet at Massey," the social media campaign celebrated live music's

◂ Feist and the Tragically Hip played as part of the 2021 JUNOS broadcast, making them the first artists to perform in the newly refurbished Allan Slaight Auditorium.

Jesse Kumagai, current president and CEO of the Corporation of Massey Hall and Roy Thomson Hall, looks forward to expanding the not-for-profit's focus on artist development, education, and outreach.

return to Toronto by revealing the hall's first slate of concerts. To no one's surprise, a trio of nights by Mr. Lightfoot were the inaugural shows (November 25–27).

Other artists announced included many Canadians — and past performers — such as Bruce Cockburn, Jann Arden, Whitehorse, William Prince with Serena Ryder, and Buffy Sainte-Marie with the Sadies. Joining these veterans were a slew of artists ready to make their Massey Hall debuts such as the Glorious Sons with a three-night run and Broken Social Scene, whose show would be the first to feature the general admission floor. Ticket sales were brisk. Many of the shows sold out within days of their announcements, showing the public's appetite for the return of live music and the reopening of their beloved hall.

President and CEO Jesse Kumagai said this announcement felt like a homecoming for so many artists whose music helped shape the legacy of the venue. When the hall shut for refurbishment in 2018, no one could have predicted how difficult that period would become. In early 2020, just as Kumagai was appointed president and CEO, the coronavirus was declared a global pandemic. Construction work on Massey Hall halted. Uncertainty about the future of the live-music industry loomed large.

To say Covid-19 affected the music industry is an understatement. Independent live-music venues closed at an alarming rate. In Toronto alone, twenty-two venues were lost and many more placed in precarious positions. An industry already hit hard by rising real estate prices, along with increased government regulations and property taxes, was on life support. The silver lining: as we all entered prolonged periods of self-isolation, so many of us learned how integral art is to our mental health and our ability to cope in times of turmoil. However, no streamed show from an artist's living room could replace the feeling of a shared live experience in a favourite venue, and the uncertainty of when the pandemic would end weighed heavily on everyone's mind.

Massey Hall was initially scheduled to have its grand opening sometime in the final quarter of 2020, a date that came and went as the entire world dealt with the crisis. But as Kumagai said at the time,

> We have a great deal of confidence people will come back. That positions us to open as a beacon of hope for people and a sign of things returning to some sense of normalcy. By the time we open, the music community will judge the renovations. There has obviously been concern about us being reverent of this important cultural asset and that we are not doing anything to destroy it [during the revitalization]. A lot of people were concerned it would be sterilized through the refurbishment. I admit that initially I was a little worried about that, too, but when you see the new building you realize it's still Massey Hall.

"Everything a show should be is what happens each time we play Massey. The reception we get from the audience is awesome; it is the rock 'n roll Carnegie Hall of Canada. It's flawless. That is why we keep coming back."

— George Thorogood, blues musician and leader of George Thorogood & The Destroyers

Despite the vulnerability of venues and the economic impact of the pandemic on the live-music sector, the Massey Hall Forever capital campaign that former CEO and president Deane Cameron had championed continued. In late 2020, the Slaight Family Foundation announced an additional five million dollars would be donated to the Massey Hall Revitalization Project, for a total donation of ten million dollars. To acknowledge the foundation's tremendous support, the venue's stage and auditorium were renamed in honour of Allan Slaight.

Before the end of the year, one more major donation was announced from Allied Properties. The partnership with the urban developer would expand the revitalization's original scope and turn the complex into Canada's premiere multi-purpose performance facility — the Allied Music Centre — now home of historic Massey Hall. "We are immeasurably grateful for this remarkable gift to Canada's music scene," said Kumagai. The Allied Music Centre features new state-of-the-art performance venues and dedicated spaces for artist development, education,

An artist's rendering of the revitalized Massey Hall, including the brand-new attached Allied Music Centre building, which will feature an additional venue, a dedicated space for artists, a recording studio, and much more.

and outreach initiatives, all located in the seven-storey tower adjacent to the hall itself. A new recording studio within the centre was named after the late, beloved leader of Massey Hall, Deane Cameron. Following the announcement, friends and the Canadian music community were encouraged to share their favourite memories of Deane and honour his legacy by donating to the studio.

• • •

Hart Massey wanted the hall he built in downtown Toronto to be a place for the people and a lasting legacy. The theme that rang out during my research for this book over the last three years is that, despite the pandemic, the Grand Old Lady of Shuter Street remains a place where people look forward to congregating. As the new and improved Massey Hall reopens with a more modern look and upgraded amenities to serve artists and patrons, the leadership, led by Kumagai, still follows Hart's vision and honours his gift.

But, many questions still remain. What will the post–Covid-19 world look like when it comes to live music? Will audiences still have the same appetite to attend a show, sitting in intimate proximity to strangers in a 2,500-person concert hall? Some of the fears that stemmed from the pandemic, where people learned to social distance and quarantine, will definitely linger, but for how long? Only time will tell.

What the pandemic did teach us is how important these live experiences are — especially the longer we lived without them. Massey Hall stands tall. Rejuvenated. Ready to welcome a new generation of listeners and old friends to its congregation to celebrate with song and musical communion at the altar of this music temple. A new version of the Canadian landmark shines. Hart Massey would approve. Long live live music. Massey Hall forever.

# Acknowledgements

I am humbled that I had the chance to write this history of Massey Hall, and I hope I succeeded in capturing the soul and cultural significance of this iconic building.

Deciding what to include in a history of a building that has witnessed so much over the years was one of the most difficult tasks. A valuable starting point was William Kilbourn's well-researched book, *Intimate Grandeur: One Hundred Years of Massey Hall*, published to mark the hall's centennial in 1994. This secondary source painted a picture of Massey Hall through the eyes of another historian. It allowed me to decide how I would begin to fill my canvas, and it was a constant reference during the three years I spent researching and writing this book. I relied on guidance from the artists who have been lucky enough to stand on that storied stage — I asked questions, heard their stories, and sifted through them looking for common threads. Slowly, all the reasons why Massey Hall is such an incredible venue emerged. I spent hundreds of hours losing myself down various rabbit holes, poring through the Massey Hall archives (thanks, Ashley D'Andrea) and those of the City of Toronto, through old issues of the *Globe and Mail* and *Toronto Star*

— all these sources led me to discover many new stories and facts to add to this narrative. Thanks to the following libraries for providing access to these invaluable online databases: the Toronto Public Library, Kitchener Public Library, and Wilfrid Laurier library.

The shows I've seen at Massey over the decades are too many to count but include the Pretenders, Annie Lennox, Loretta Lynn, Lucinda Williams, Barenaked Ladies, Blue Rodeo, John Prine, Daniel Lanois, and the legendary Gordon Lightfoot. At each show, I felt the mystique and the gravitas of this great hall. I've seen shows with friends and shows with my wife. I've also attended many concerts alone, on assignment, writing reviews for various publications. And I shared many of my favourite Massey experiences with my dad, most memorably seeing Neil Young during his *Chrome Dreams II* tour (2007) and Jackson Browne (2011), who appeared alone on stage with dozens of acoustic guitars and a pair of pianos, taking requests from the audience and showcasing the hall's intimacy.

I'd like to acknowledge you, the reader, for your support of and interest in Massey Hall over the years, whether by buying a ticket to a show or picking up a copy of this book.

Thank you to my family for their ongoing support, love, and encouragement. Thanks to my mom, dad, and sister, who have always championed my writing, supported my career choice, and believed in me. Writing a book is not easy. It requires sacrifice. My wife, Patricia, is my constant companion on life's journey. She is my daily inspiration and my muse. *Gracias, corazón*. I love you *para siempre*. To my children, Alex and Isabella, I'm so grateful for the joy you bring to my life. Your encouragement is valued more than you know. You, too, have always supported my work and championed my writing whenever self-doubt crept in. Your encouragement is valued more than you know.

Every picture tells a story, indeed. The photographs I carefully curated throughout this book showcase Massey Hall's illustrious history as much as the words I've written to tell this story. Thank you to all of the photographers whose work is included in the book. I'm forever grateful for your contributions. Special thanks goes to Richard Beland and John Rowlands, who went above and beyond — donating countless amazing pictures to this labour of love. Thanks also to the photographers who documented Massey Hall over the years and who agreed to having so many of their beautiful shots in the book, including Jag Gundu, Salina Kassam, and Matt Barnes.

I would also be remiss if I did not credit all of the amazing artist managers and publicists who arranged interviews and provided photographs from their artists. There are too many names to list here, but know that I'm grateful to each of you for the part you played in this project.

Thank you to the Dundurn Press team, past and present: from founder, past president, and publisher emeritus Kirk Howard (who retired and sold the business in 2019 to a consortium of tech entrepreneurs led by Randall Howard, Lorne Wallace, and Jason Martin) to current president and publisher Scott Fraser. Following the success of my first book, *The Legendary Horseshoe Tavern: A Complete History*, they accepted my proposal for this project and supported me throughout the process. Though the book was originally scheduled for fall 2020 publication, the pandemic — and ensuing economic recession — forced us to push the date to the following year. Special mention is due to associate publisher Kathryn Lane, who gave me early feedback on my initial drafts and met with me many times throughout the writing to help refine and reframe the book's structure. I was also lucky to once again work with editor extraordinaire Allison Hirst. She helped take my words and vision and reorganize them to make the stories come alive. Her input was invaluable and I'm grateful for her guidance. Final thanks to my publisher's team goes to copy editor Jess Shulman, who received the manuscript in its home stretch; her input and eagle eye (including checking nearly nine hundred proper nouns) were invaluable to the finished book you now hold in your hands. Thanks also to art director Laura Boyle, managing editor Elena Radic, and publicist Heather Wood.

Thanks also to the Ontario Arts Council for their financial support of this project. Their funding helped cover some of my travel expenses to and from Toronto from my hometown in Waterloo to interview artists and conduct research at the Massey Hall archive, City of Toronto archives, and the Toronto Reference Library.

Gratitude goes to the leaders at Massey Hall — especially the late Deane Cameron (president and CEO of the Corporation of Massey Hall and Roy Thomson Hall, 2015 to 2019), current president and CEO Jesse Kumagai, and communications manager Mima Agozzino. These individuals trusted me from our first meeting, helping and guiding me every step of the way on this journey. Deane led this most recent revitalization and leaves an extremely important legacy. I was fortunate to befriend him and spend some time with him during my time researching and writing this book. Without the help, support, and encouragement of Deane, Jesse, Mima, and the rest of the Massey Hall team I worked with, especially Cathie Carlino, Ashley D'Andrea, Stephen McGrath, Grant Troop, and Doug McKendrick, this book would not have happened. Deane championed my project and helped me every step of the way by facilitating interviews, making suggestions for storylines to follow, sharing his knowledge and passion for the hall, and granting access to the corporation's archives. He even gave me his seat on the floor so I could witness Gordon Lightfoot close the venue on Canada Day 2018 before the renovations. I was saddened by Deane's death in the summer of 2019, by the fact that he will be unable to see his vision completed and be there for the reopening. At his funeral, held at Roy Thomson Hall (RTH), his long-time friend Tom Cochrane sang "The Weight" — the classic tune by the Band, who was performing the first time Tom and Deane went to Massey together as teenagers. It was extremely moving as, unrehearsed, and as the mourners that filled the lower bowl at RTH sang along, several other artists, including Damhnait Doyle and Serena Ryder, bounded down the aisles and joined Tom for a sing-a-long to what happens to be my favourite song. Talk about chills. I know Deane is up there, along with the other artists who have gone before. His spirit is in the revitalized hall and I know he is smiling knowing his work is done and his beloved hall has reopened and is ready to serve a new generation of music lovers.

And finally, thank you, Hart Massey, for your 1894 gift to Toronto, to Canada, and to the world. Your gift keeps giving and enriching so many lives with the variety of programming behind those three red doors.

# Sources

## A Note About Sources

As I researched and wrote this book, I relied primarily on first-person interviews with artists who had played the hall, promoters, members of the music industry — past and present — and media members who have covered shows there. I also made use of Massey Hall's archives, the City of Toronto archives, Library and Archives Canada, and the Toronto Public Library. I also relied heavily on the archives of the *Toronto Star* and the *Globe and Mail*.

## Bibliography

Barclay, Michael. *The Never-ending Present: The Story of Gord Downie and The Tragically Hip* (Toronto: ECW Press, 2018).

Barclay, Michael, Ian Jack, and Jason Schneider. *Have Not Been The Same: The Canrock Renaissance 1985–1995*, tenth anniversary edition (Toronto: ECW Press, 2011).

Bazzana, Kevin. *Wondrous Strange: The Life and Arts of Glenn Gould* (Toronto: McClelland & Stewart, 2003).

Bidini, Dave. *Around the World in 57 1/2 Gigs* (Toronto: McClelland & Stewart, 2007).

Bidini, Dave. *On a Cold Road: Tales of Adventure in Canadian Rock* (Toronto: McClelland & Stewart, 1998).

Bidini, Dave. *Writing Gordon Lightfoot* (Toronto: McClelland & Stewart, 2011).

Cockburn, Bruce. *Rumours of Glory: A Memoir* (Toronto: HarperOne, 2014).

Collins, Paul. *The Canadians: Hart Massey* (Toronto: Fitzhenry & Whiteside, 1977).
Connors, Stompin' Tom. *Stompin' Tom and the Connors Tone* (Toronto: Viking, 2000).
Filey, Mike. "Our Massey Hall Turns 100." In *Toronto Sketches 3: The Way We Were.* (Toronto: Dundurn Press, 1994).
Finkelstein, Bernie. *True North: A Life in the Music Business* (Toronto: McClelland & Stewart, 2012).
Goddard, John, and Richard Crouse. *Rock and Roll Toronto: From Alanis to Zeppelin* (Toronto: Doubleday Canada Limited, 1997).
Goddard, Peter. *The Great Gould* (Toronto: Dundurn Press, 2017).
Jennings, Nicholas. *Before the Gold Rush: Flashbacks to the Dawn of the Canadian Sound* (Toronto: Viking, 1997).
Jennings, Nicholas. *Lightfoot* (Toronto: Penguin Random House, 2017).
Kilbourn, William. *Intimate Grandeur: One Hundred Years at Massey Hall* (Toronto: Stoddart, 1993).
Mersereau, Bob. *The History of Canadian Rock 'n' Roll* (Milwaukee: Backbeat Books, 2015).
Robertson, Robbie. *Testimony* (Toronto: Penguin Random House/Knopf Canada, 2016).
Schneider, Jason. *Whispering Pines: The Northern Roots of American Music … From Hank Snow to the Band* (Toronto: ECW Press, 2009).
Young, Scott. *Neil & Me* (Toronto: McClelland & Stewart, 1997).
Various authors. *Shine a Light*, no. 2 (Massey Hall Corporation, 2018).

## Videos/TV

"History Behind Toronto's Massey Hall." *Rewind: CityNews*. April 28, 2016 (originally aired in 1981).
Hobbs, Greg. "Massey Hall Memories." *CBC News/The National*. June 13, 2018.
McDonald, Bruce. "Geddy Lee (Rush) at Massey Hall." 2009. kensingtontv.com/citysonic/films/Geddy-Lee-Rush-at-Massey-Hall.php.

## LPs, Liner Notes, Albums

Bruce Cockburn, *Circles in the Stream*, True North, 1977; liner notes written by Nicholas Jennings.
Crowbar, *Crowbar: Live!* Daffodil Records, 1970.
*The Quintet, Jazz at Massey Hall*, Debut Records, 1953; liner notes written by Bill Coss.
Rush, *All the World's a Stage*, Mercury Records, 1976.
Neil Young, *Neil Young: Live at Massey Hall*, Reprise, 1972.

## Websites

masseyhall.com; jonimitchell.com

## Interviews

- Jann Arden, March 12, 2019
- Matt Andersen, February 4, 2019
- Randy Bachman, January 11, 2019
- Jack Batten, April 11, 2019
- Nancy Beaton, January 25, 2019
- Katie Beaton, February 1, 2021
- Rob Bennett, December 27, 2018
- Sonnie Bernardi, August 1, 2019
- Dave Bidini, March 8, 2019
- Rob Bowman, October 29, 2018
- Deane Cameron, December 7, 2018
- David Clayton-Thomas, December 4, 2018
- Tom Cochrane, February 21, 2019
- Bruce Cockburn, December 10, 2018
- Pablo Coffey, January 11, 2019
- Jeff Cohen, December 7, 2020
- Lena Connors, January 23, 2019
- Tom Connors Jr., January 23, 2019
- Gary Cormier, May 25, 2019
- Gary Craig, March 20, 2019
- Jim Cuddy, November 13, 2018
- Burton Cummings, August 13, 2019
- Ellen Davidson, November 16, 2018
- Frank Davies, November 1, 2018
- John Derringer, January 11, 2019
- Bruce Dickinson, April 12, 2019
- Bob Doidge, April 8, 2019
- John Donabie, October 23, 2018
- Bazil Donovan, December 29, 2018
- Denise Donlon, November 20, 2018
- Luke Doucet, January 8, 2019
- Brian Edwards, January 24, 2019
- Bob Essert, March 9, 2020
- Mary Anne Farrell, December 14, 2018
- Bernie Fiedler, December 5, 2018
- Bernie Finkelstein, October 31, 2018
- Richard Flohil, October 23, 2018
- Sue Foley, December 19, 2018
- Ray Furlotte, March 19, 2020
- Ian Gilchrist, February 6, 2019
- Peter Goddard, January 22, 2019
- Jake Gold, January 16, 2019
- Bruce Good, January 16, 2019
- Lawrence Gowan, March 6, 2019
- Sharon Hampson, October 23, 2018
- Kevin Hearn, December 14, 2018
- Amy Helm, May 1, 2019
- Dan Hill, January 21, 2021
- Andrea Iscoe, November 27, 2018
- iskwē, June 9, 2020
- Molly Johnson, January 29, 2021
- Kevin Kane, October 18, 2018
- Steve Kane, December 3, 2018
- Peter Katz, February 4, 2021
- Barry Keane, October 22, 2018
- Greg Keelor, May 1, 2020
- Geoffrey Kelly, February 2, 2021
- Andy Kim, December 28, 2018
- Bill King, October 29, 2018
- Jesse Kumagai, February 3, 2021
- Robbie Lane, October 22, 2020
- Craig Laskey, November 23, 2020
- Geddy Lee, January 29, 2019
- Elliott Lefko, October 18, 2018
- Gordon Lightfoot, December 12, 2018
- Colin Linden, October 26, 2018
- Matt Mays, January 15, 2019
- Doug McClement, February 6, 2019
- Stephen McGrath, January 26, 2021
- Doug McKendrick, August 29, 2019

- Murray McLauchlan, November 20, 2018
- Mark Miller, December 13, 2018
- Bram Morrison, October 23, 2018
- Nana Mouskouri, March 23, 2019
- Miranda Mulholland, May 31, 2019
- Anne Murray, November 26, 2020
- Paul Myers, January 10, 2019
- Riley O'Connor, February 28, 2019
- Joel Plaskett, December 21, 2020
- Ed Preston, March 15, 2019
- Dave Prowse, November 12, 2020
- Ed Robertson, January 18, 2019
- Robbie Robertson, January 22, 2019
- Duff Roman, November 26, 2018
- Bob Roper, June 5, 2020
- Shakura S'Aida, February 3, 2021
- Lorraine Segato, January 18, 2021
- Ron Sexsmith, November 24, 2018
- Shad, February 17, 2021
- Jane Siberry, April 5, 2019
- Gord Sinclair, April 6, 2020
- Vanessa Smith, February 2, 2021
- Steve Stanley, December 7, 2018
- Kevan Staples, January 21, 2021
- John Stirratt, May 2, 2019
- George Stroumboulopoulos, February 7, 2019
- Jill Taylor, February 2, 2021
- Pat Taylor, February 5, 2021
- George Thorogood, April 25, 2019
- Gary Topp, June 1, 2020
- Grant Troop, April 28, 2021
- Valdy, January 28, 2019
- Sharon Vattay, March 19, 2020
- Rufus Wainwright, February 14, 2019
- Christopher Ward, December 12, 2018
- Steve Waxman, January 9, 2019
- Jörn Weisbrodt, February 14, 2019
- Tom Wilson (of Little Caesar and the Consuls), October 25, 2018
- Tom Wilson (of Junkhouse, Lee Harvey Osmond, and Blackie and the Rodeo Kings), January 25, 2019
- Royal Wood, January 26, 2019
- Cal Woodruff, February 8, 2021

# Notes

## Introduction: Massey Hall Forever

1. Timothy Luginbuhl, "My Massey Memory – Vincent Massey Tovell [video interview]," YouTube, January 30, 2016, youtube.com/watch?v=H_1oyHWMHaA.
2. A selection of other artists who have recorded at Massey Hall over the years include Chuck Mangione, the Chieftains, Ronnie Hawkins, Matthew Good, Pavlo, and "Weird Al" Yankovic.

## Chapter 1: The House That Hart Built

1. "A Great Public Hall," *Globe*, December 5, 1892, 2.
2. Withrow was also a founding partner in Withrow and Hillock, building contractors and lumber merchants, specializing in wooden sashes and doors. Withrow and Hillock did the carpentry work and supplied the doors and sashes for Massey Hall. Withrow was the first chair of the Board of Trustees that operated the hall, and during his lifetime he was the only non-Massey trustee. See "Withrow, John Jacob," *Dictionary of Canadian Biography,* 1990, biographi.ca/en/bio/withrow_john_jacob_12E.html.
3. S.M. Creighton, *The Story of Massey Hall*, 1934.
4. "Badgley, Sidney Rose," Biographical Dictionary of Architects in Canada 1800–1950, dictionaryofarchitectsincanada.org/node/1020.
5. William Kilbourn, *Intimate Grandeur: One Hundred Years at Massey Hall* (Toronto: Stoddart, 1993), 21.
6. Andrea Yu, "Massey Hall: Past, Present and Proposed Future," Urban Toronto, May 7, 2013; urbantoronto.ca/news/2013/05/massey-hall-past-present-and-proposed-future.
7. "General News of the City," *Globe*, April 21, 1893, 8.
8. Brad Wheeler, "The Top 10 Most Significant Concerts in Massey Hall's History, as Reviewed

by The Globe," *Globe and Mail*, June 27, 2018, theglobeandmail.com/arts/music/article-top-10-most-significant-massey-hall-concerts.

9. Pierre Berton, "There'll Always be a Massey," *Maclean's*, October 15, 1951, archive.macleans.ca/article/1951/10/15/therell-always-be-a-massey.
10. David Roberts, "Massey, Hart Almerrin," in *Dictionary of Canadian Biography*, vol. 12 (University of Toronto/Université Laval, 2003–), biographi.ca/en/bio/massey_hart_almerrin_12E.html.
11. G. B. van Blaricom, "Revolutionizing an Industry," *The Busy Man's Magazine* XVII, no. 5 (March 1, 1909), available at archive.macleans.ca/article/1909/3/1/revolutionizing-an-industry.
12. Joseph Lindsey, "Hart Almerrin Massey," *Canadian Encyclopedia*, May 28, 2018, thecanadianencyclopedia.ca/en/article/hart-almerrin-massey.
13. Paul Collins, *Hart Massey (The Canadians).* (Don Mills, Ontario: Fitzhenry & Whiteside, 1977), Chapter 11.
14. Most of the early famed musicians and orators that took the stage at Massey Hall entertained first at Euclid Hall.
15. Lucy Booth, *Toronto: 100 Years of Grandeur: The Inside Stories of Toronto's Great Homes and the People Who Lived There* (Toronto: Pagurian Press, 1978).
16. Berton, "There'll Always be a Massey."
17. Kilbourn, *Intimate Grandeur*, 19.
18. Paul Collins, *Hart Massey (The Canadians)*, Chapter 11.

### Chapter 2: The Early Years: Opening Night to the Great Depression

1. Kilbourn, *Intimate Grandeur*, 5.
2. Kilbourn, *Intimate Grandeur*, 47.
3. Kilbourn, *Intimate Grandeur*, 47–48.
4. "Attendance Required," Toronto Mendelssohn Choir, January 16, 2018, tmchoir.org/attendance-required.
5. Kilbourn, *Intimate Grandeur*, 48.
6. "Moody's Farewell: The Evangelist Concludes His Work in Toronto," *Globe*, November 26, 1894, 8.
7. *Sherlock Holmes in Toronto: Conan Doyle's Massey Hall Lecture 26 November 1894*, Toronto Reference Library, 1980. Found in the Arthur Conan Doyle Room.
8. "Mr. Churchill on the War," *Globe*, December 31, 1900, 7.
9. "The Negro and His Future: Booker T. Washington on the Race Problem," *Globe*, November 27, 1902, 10.
10. Edward VII ascended to the throne in 1902, following Queen Victoria's death in 1901.

11. Arthur Milnes, "Once Upon a City: Massey Hall's Importance to Politics," *Toronto Star*, October 28, 2015.
12. Kevin Plummer, "Historicist: The Horses Reign," *Torontoist*, March 8, 2014, torontoist.com/2014/03/historicist-the-horses-reign.
13. Kilbourn, *Intimate Grandeur*, 77.
14. Richard S. Warren, *Begins with the Oboe*: *A History of the Toronto Symphony Orchestra* (Toronto: University of Toronto Press, 2002), 11.
15. "CityNews Rewind: A Look Back at the Historic Bond between the TSO and Massey Hall [video]," CityNews, May 12, 2016, toronto.citynews.ca/video/2016/05/12/citynews-rewind-a-look-back-at-the-historic-bond-between-the-tso-and-massey-hall.
16. Kilbourn, *Intimate Grandeur*, 78.
17. Officially the Canadian National Railways Radio Department, in the 1920s the CNR was the short-lived first attempt at a national radio network.
18. Warren, *Begins with the Oboe*, 18.
19. "Massey Hall at 100: A Centennial to Celebrate," *Globe*, Saturday, June 4, 1994.
20. "Moving Message from World of Darkness," *Globe*, January 10, 1914.
21. *The Beaver* 87, no. 1 (February–March 2007): 10.
22. "Music and the Drama: Massey Hall. Jazz Artillery of Paul Whiteman Captivates a Huge Audience" *Globe*, October 2, 1924, 13.
23. E.R. Parkhurst, "Music and the Drama: Caruso Breaks All Records Office Receipts: Greatest in Massey History," *Globe*, October 1, 1920, 9; "Caruso Has Arrived: The Great Tenor's First Visit to Toronto," *Globe*, May 4, 1908, 12.
24. Kilbourn, *Intimate Grandeur*, 81.
25. Kilbourn, *Intimate Grandeur*, 82.
26. Kilbourn, *Intimate Grandeur*, 82.

### Chapter 3: The Jazz Age and Beyond

1. "Clock Prince Consulted Now Graces Massey Hall," *Globe*, October 16, 1933, 11.
2. "Alterations Made at Massey Hall," *Globe*, June 23, 1933, 11; Kilbourn, *Intimate Grandeur*, 84–85.
3. See Chapter 13 for more on Ernest MacMillan.
4. Warren, *Begins with the Oboe*, 22.
5. "Hockey Arena Not 'The Tops' To Whiteman: King of Jazz Looks Lonely in Vast Oval — Prefers Massey Hall," *Globe and Mail*, October 10, 1938, 21.
6. Jamie Bradburn, "Vintage Toronto Ads: Oscar Peterson," *Torontoist*, June 2015.
7. Dillon O'Leary, "Swing Pianist Stirs Massey Hall Throng," *Globe and Mail*, March 8, 1946, 21.

8. Alex Barris, "Louis Rocks 'Em Black and Blue; Five Friends Help," *Globe and Mail*, May 20, 1949, 12.
9. William Krehm, "Massey Hall Reopening Marked by Beethoven's Consecration," *Globe and Mail*, September 29, 1949, 13.
10. Frank Tumpane, "At City Hall," *Globe and Mail*, August 25, 1944, 3.
11. Kilbourn, *Intimate Grandeur*, 123.
12. "All Quiet at Massey Hall as Toronto Reds Mourn," *Globe and Mail*, March 10, 1953, 5.
13. "A Look at One of Mississauga's Most Influential Women," InSauga, March 6, 2020, insauga.com/a-look-at-one-of-mississaugas-most-influential-women.
14. "My Day" newspaper column, The Eleanor Roosevelt Papers, May 19, 1955, gwu.edu/~erpapers/myday/displaydoc.cfm?_y=1955&_f=md003173.
15. John Doug Taylor, "Toronto's Old Movie Theatres — The Infamous Casino on Queen St.," Historic Toronto, November 6, 2013, tayloronhistory.com/2013/11/06/torontos-old-movie-theatresthe-infamous-casino-on-queen-st.
16. Mark Miller, "A Night to Remember," *Globe and Mail*, May 10, 2003.
17. Mark Miller, *Cool Blues: Charlie Parker in Canada 1953* (Nightwood Editions, 1990), 49.
18. "Heath, Ted," eJazz Lines: The Global Source for Jazz, ejazzlines.com/big-band-arrangements/by-performer/heath-ted/.
19. Geoff Pevere, "Toronto Pop Chronicles: The Greatest Jazz Concert Ever?" *Toronto Star,* July 8, 2011.
20. Alex Barris, "Home Talent Holds Own with U.S. Jazz Stars," *Globe and Mail*, May 18, 1953, 8.
21. RJ Smith, "50 Greatest Live Albums of All Time," *Rolling Stone*, April 29, 2015.
22. Bill King, "The Greatest Jazz Concert Ever: A 1992 Interview with Drummer Max Roach," FYI Music News, November 2, 2018, fyimusicnews.ca/articles/2018/11/02/greatest-jazz-concert-ever-1992-interview-drummer-max-roach.
23. Bill Coss, in the liner notes from *The Quintet, Jazz at Massey Hall* (Debut Records: 1953).

### Chapter 4: For Folk's Sake: The 1960s

1. Kilbourn, *Intimate Grandeur*, 119.
2. "Toronto Feature: O'Keefe Centre," *Canadian Encyclopedia*, thecanadianencyclopedia.ca/en/article/toronto-feature-okeefe-centre.
3. "Restoring a Masterpiece," Mirvish, mirvish.com/restoring-a-masterpiece.
4. Gino Francesconi, "How to Deflect a Wrecking Ball with a Violin," New York Public Radio, Nov 6, 2014, wnyc.org/story/saving-carnegie-hall-wrecking-ball.
5. Betty Lee, "The Plan for a New Massey Hall," *Globe and Mail*, October 3, 1970, 21.
6. Kilbourn, *Intimate Grandeur*, 120–21.
7. "Home of the Great, Massey Hall Doomed," *Globe and Mail*, October 13, 1967, 1.

8. Betty Lee, "The Plan for a New Massey Hall," *Globe and Mail*, October 3, 1970, 21.
9. Kilbourn, *Intimate Grandeur*, 121.
10. Taken from this video interview: "Geddy Lee (Rush) at Massey Hall," dir. Bruce McDonald (2009), kensingtontv.com/citysonic/films/Geddy-Lee-Rush-at-Massey-Hall.php.
11. "Massey Music Hall and TMC," Toronto Mendelssohn Choir, July 18, 2019, tmchoir.org/massey-music-hall-and-tmc.
12. Bruce Lawson, "A Changed Bob Dylan Booed in Toronto," *Globe and Mail*, November 16, 1965.
13. Jamie Bradburn, "Review of Bob Dylan's Performance at Massey Hall, the Telegram, November 15, 1965," *Torontoist*, July 30, 2013, torontoist.com/2013/07/the-old-lady-of-shuter-street/20130730dylanreview.
14. Robbie Robertson, *Testimony* (Toronto: Knopf Canada, 2016); plus author interview.
15. Robertson, *Testimony*, 191.
16. Robertson, *Testimony*, 193.

## Chapter 5: Let There Be Rock: The 1970s

1. Kilbourn, *Intimate Grandeur*, 120.
2. Anne Murray with Michael Posner, *All of Me* (Knopf Canada, 2009), 89; plus author interview.
3. Tom Connors, *Stompin' Tom and the Connors Tone* (Toronto: Viking Canada, 2000).
4. Johnny Dovercourt, *Any Night of the Week: A D.I.Y. History of Toronto Music 1957–2001* (Toronto: Coach House Books, 2020), 35.
5. Bill King, "Marley, Massey Hall & the Kings!," FYI Music News, September 7, 2018, fyimusicnews.ca/articles/2018/09/07/marley-massey-hall-kings.

## Chapter 6: The 1980s

1. Paul McGrath, "Police Get Down to Reggae Roots," *Globe and Mail*, November 26, 1980; Dan Hamilton, "Peroxide Blondes Bust Loose at Massey," *Eye*, November 27, 1980, 18; Wilder Penfield III, "Police's Explosive Concert Creates Concert Frenzy," *Toronto Sun*, November 26, 1980.
2. Peter Goddard, "Sharon, Lois, Bram Bridge Generation Gap," *Toronto Star*, December 9, 1985, C3.
3. Bill King, "A Conversation with … Jane Siberry," FYI Music News, May 20, 2016, fyimusicnews.ca/articles/2016/05/20/conversation-jane-siberry.

## Chapter 7: Canadians Take Centre Stage: The 1990s

1. "Lewis, Perkins Turn Up to Mark Hawkins' 60th," *Edmonton Journal*, January 14, 1995, F2; Nick Krewen, "Legends Help Hawk Mark his 60th Birthday," *Spectator*, January 13, 1995, D4.

### Chapter 8: The New Millennium

1. Danny Murray, "Massey Hall Presents 50th Anniversary Concert the Quintet," Minnesota Blues, May 15, 2003, mnblues.com/review/2003/masseyhall-50th503-dm.html.
2. "Jazz Stories at Massey Hall," Massey Hall and Roy Thomson Hall, masseyhallandroythomsonhall.com/our-history/masseyhall/jazz-stories-at-massey-hall/.
3. Ben Rayner, "'It Was Electric' — Musicians Share Their Top Massey Hall Memories Before It Closes," *Toronto Star,* June 29, 2018.

### Chapter 9: The House of Gord

1. Peter Goddard, "Lightfoot Marks Time with Surface Hipness," *Globe and Mail*, March 31, 1967, 16.

### Chapter 10: Last Call at the Hall

1. Nick Patch, "Gord Downie, the Sadies' Joint Release the Result of a Long, Long Collaboration," *Canadian Press*, April 16, 2014, 570news.com/2014/04/16/gord-downie-the-sadies-joint-release-the-result-of-a-long-long-collaboration/.
2. David McPherson, "Review: *Neil Young Journeys* Premieres in Toronto," *American Songwriter*, 2011, americansongwriter.com/review-neil-young-journeys-premieres-in-canada/.
3. Kevin Naulis, "Justin Bieber's Massey Hall Christmas Concert Sells Out in 30 Minutes (Prepare to Be Gouged by Scalpers)," *Toronto Life*, December 19, 2011, torontolife.com/city/justin-bieber-massey-hall-christmas-concert/; "Fans Wild for Bieber's Toronto Show," CP24, December 21, 2011, cp24.com/fans-wild-for-bieber-s-toronto-show-1.743342.
4. Victoria Ahearn, "Russell Peters on Netflix Special, Meeting Syrian Refugees, Political Correctness," 660 City News, April 21, 2016, 660citynews.com/2016/04/21/russell-peters-on-netflix-special-meeting-syrian-refugees-political-correctness.
5. Brad Wheeler, "The Top 10 Most Significant Concerts in Massey Hall's History, reviewed by the *Globe*," *Globe and Mail*, June 27, 2018, theglobeandmail.com/arts/music/article-top-10-most-significant-massey-hall-concerts; plus author interviews.
6. Blue Rodeo also previously recorded its *Blue Road* album there (2008).

### Chapter 11: Revitalization

1. Shawn Micallef, "Windows to the Sky," *Shine a Light* (Massey Hall publication) no. 2 (2018), 12–14.
2. Micallef, "Windows to the Sky," 12–14.
3. Marshall Long, "What Is So Special About Shoebox Halls? Envelopment, Envelopment, Envelopment," *Acoustics Today* 3, no. 2 (Spring 2009): 23
4. The beginning of architectural acoustics as a science began at Harvard University's Fogg

Art Museum in the late nineteenth century. Since the lecture hall had inadequate acoustics, American physicist Wallace Clement Sabine was tasked with discovering why. Sabine tested the acoustics of the room using a stopwatch and a number of seat cushions, formulating an equation for reverberation time. He was the first to quantify and measure factors that contribute to room acoustics, and as a result, the unit for a material's sound absorption — the sabine — is named after him; see "The Acoustics Behind the World's Most Renowned Concert Halls," Invaluable, May 22, 2019, invaluable.com/blog/acoustics-behind-concert-halls.

5. Wheeler, "The Top 10 Most Significant Concerts in Massey Hall's History, as Reviewed by the *Globe*."
6. Kilbourn, *Intimate Grandeur*, 1.
7. Timothy Andrew McIntosh and Patricia Wardrop Maloney, "Massey Hall," *Canadian Encyclopedia*, August 29, 2013 (last updated July 24, 2018), thecanadianencyclopedia.ca/en/article/massey-hall.
8. King, "A Conversation with … Jane Siberry."
9. Chris Bateman, "How Toronto Turned a Rail Yard into Roy Thomson Hall," *blogTO*, September 28, 2013, blogto.com/city/2013/09/how_toronto_turned_a_rail_yard_in_to_roy_thomson_hall.
10. Long, "What is So Special about Shoebox Halls? Envelopment, Envelopment, Envelopment," 22.
11. "Concert Hall Acoustics Influence the Emotional Impact of Music," Aalto University, March 23, 2016, aalto.fi/en/news/concert-hall-acoustics-influence-the-emotional-impact-of-music.
12. Andrew King, "The Sound Matches the Stature: A New Audio System and New Era at Toronto's Massey Hall," *Professional Sound* XXVIII, no. 3 (June 2017).
13. King, "The Sound Matches the Stature."
14. Barbara Carss, "Massey Hall Burnished for New Generations," Canadian Facility Management and Design, October 16, 2019, reminetwork.com/articles/massey-hall-burnished-new-generations.
15. Paul Comeau, "Acoustically Speaking," *Shine A Light*, no. 2 (2017).

## Chapter 12: Artist Development and Outreach

1. In 2021, the songwriter released a live record documenting this milestone.
2. Nordicity, *Re:Venues — A Case and Path Forward for Toronto's Live Music Industry*, Canadian Live Music Association, 2020, 5, canadianlivemusic.ca/wp-content/uploads/2020/10/Re-Venues-FINAL-REPORT.pdf.
3. Luke Ottenhof, "Husband and Wife Duo Tackle Historic Venue," *Charlatan*, February 27, 2003.
4. Corporation of Massey Hall and Roy Thomson Hall Annual Report 2016–2017.
5. Corporation of Massey Hall and Roy Thomson Hall Annual Report 2013–2014, 13.

6. Annual Report 2013–14, 13.
7. Celebrated writer and activist June Callwood helped launch Jessie's: The June Callwood Centre for Young Women (formerly Jessie's Centre for Teenagers) in downtown Toronto in 1982.

### Chapter 13: Legendary Leaders

1. Sir Ernest MacMillan: *The Importance of Being Canadian*, (University of Toronto Press, 1996), 13.
2. Kilbourn, *Intimate Grandeur*, 90.
3. Kilbourn, *Intimate Grandeur*, 91.
4. Kilbourn, *Intimate Grandeur*, 95.
5. Kilbourn, *Intimate Grandeur*, 98.
6. Charles Enman, "The Amazing MacMillan: Sir Ernest MacMillan Nurtured Canada's Musical Coming of Age," *Ottawa Citizen*, October 27, 1999, A6.
7. "Joe Cartan: From Boxing to Bach and The Band," *Globe and Mail*, September 7, 1981, M11.
8. Joe Cartan interview by Valerie Pringle, *Canada AM*, CTV Television, June 14, 1994.
9. Eric Andrew-Gee, "Massey Hall $135-million 'Revitalization' Gets Underway," *Toronto Star*, February 23, 2015.
10. Juliette Jagger quoted Cutts in an article on Massey Hall's history that appeared on the National Music Centre's website, Amplify, on August 10, 2015, amplify.nmc.ca/. The story is no longer available online.
11. Juliette Jagger, Amplify, August 10, 2015.

# Image Credits

Barnes, Matt, courtesy of Massey Hall, xiii, 110, 150, 179, 212
Beland, Richard, 18, 112, 115, 116, 118 (right), 122, 123, 127 (bottom), 128, 136, 152, 154, 182
Boyd, John, *Globe and Mail*, 53
Boyd, John, Library and Archives Canada, 11
Boyd, Liona, courtesy of 73
Bridgeman, Lorne, courtesy of Massey Hall, 214
Bridgeman Images, 34, 47, 60
Bruce, Josiah, Archives of Ontario, 17 (bottom)
Canadian Press, 74
Carnegie Hall, Susan W. Rose Archives, courtesy of, 3
Chronicle / Alamy Stock Photo, 37
Cook, Malcolm, courtesy of Massey Hall, 158, 174, 175
Coombe, Judith, 160
Crabtree, Marc, 100
Daues, Wolf-Dieter, courtesy of Terry Gadsden, 64
Davies, Frank, courtesy of, 68, 81
Davis, Barrie, *Globe and Mail*, 86
Dean, James, courtesy of the Toronto Blues Society, 197
Doubt, Scott, 135, 194
Duncan, Lindsay, 195
Emin, Alkan, xiii
Everett Collection / Bridgeman Images, 39
Everett Collection, Canadian Press, 77
Finkelstein, Bernie, courtesy of, 92 (right)
Fuda, Joseph, courtesy of Massey Hall, 5
Furlotte, Ray, 93
© Gabowicz, Fryderyk / Picture Alliance / Bridgeman Images, 107
Glenn Gould Estate, 38
Gowan, Lawrence, courtesy of, 109
Gundu, Jag, courtesy of Massey Hall, 4, 50, 127 (top), 133 (right), 137 (top & bottom), 138, 140, 141, 148, 161, 163, (bottom), 165, 171, 181, 190, 191, 199, 200, 201, 215, 220
Harrison, Leo, for *Toronto Telegram*, York University Libraries, Clara Thomas Archives & Special Collections, Toronto Telegram fonds, ASC05509, 143 (bottom)
Hearn, Kevin, courtesy of, 118 (left)
Henkenhaf, Greg, CARAS / iPhoto, 149, 218
Holland, Jac, for *Toronto Telegram*, York University Libraries, Clara Thomas Archives & Special Collections, Toronto Telegram fonds, ASC00609, 143 (top)
Hughes, Trevor, 105 (bottom)
Kassam, Salina, courtesy of Massey Hall, 124, 166, 168, 169, 172, 173, 183, 184, 208, 217
King, Bill, 129, 157
Leyes, David, 188
Library and Archives Canada, 6
Library and Archives Canada, RPM fonds, 119
Massey Hall archives, 9, 10, 12, 13, 15, 16, 20 (right), 21, 23, 24, 28, 29 (top & bottom), 30, 36, 49, 59, 94, 108 (bottom), 113, 144, 211, 222

McFadden for *Toronto Telegram* York University Libraries, Clara Thomas Archives & Special Collections, Toronto Telegram fonds, ASC06324, 41
McGinnis, Rick,147
McLorinan, Harry, *Globe and Mail*, 56, 61, 66, 85 (bottom)
© Mencarini, Marcello / Bridgeman Images, 106 (top)
Meyers, Paul, 2
Milne, Gilbert A, Archives of Ontario, 32
Mirrorpix / Courtesy Everett Collection, 106 (bottom)
Omied, Matteo / Alamy Stock Photo, 210
Pollock, Heather, courtesy of Starfish Management, 162
Rabin, Dustin, courtesy of Massey Hall, 145
Regan, Edward, *Globe and Mail*, 103
Roden, Barry, courtesy of Stompin' Tom, Ltd., 114 (bottom)
Roman, Duff, courtesy of, 72
Rowlands, John, 62, 70, 71, 76, 78, 82 (top & bottom), 84 (bottom), 85 (top), 90, 91, 146
Rowsom, Jennifer, 203, 205, 206
Salvation Army Archives, Canada and Bermuda Territory (photo 2540), used with permission, 35
Salvation Army Archives, Canada and Bermuda Territory (photo 31509), used with permission, 43
Salvation Army Archives, Canada and Bermuda Territory (photo 5775), used with permission, 58
Sandels King, Kris, 126
Sandler, Tom, 121, 161 (top)
Savoy, Valerie, 98
Sharon, Lois & Bram archives, 105 (top)
Smith, Vanessa, 204
Smith, William E. (Bill), 79
Stompin' Tom, Ltd., courtesy of, 75
Tate, Daniel / The Flyer Vault, 46, 57, 63, 84 (top), 101, 104
Terwissen, Andrew, courtesy of Massey Hall, 108 (top)
Toronto Blues Society, courtesy of, 133 (left)
Toronto Public Library, courtesy of, 8, 20 (left)
True North Records, 92 (left)
Usherson, Arthur, courtesy of Rob Bennett, 97
Waxman, Steve, 95
Wons, Nick, courtesy of Massey Hall, 153, 186
Yang, Frank,130, 132
York University Libraries, Clara Thomas Archives & Special Collections, Toronto Telegram fonds, ASC06292, 42
Zemer, Avital, courtesy of Molly Johnson, 170

# Index

*Page numbers in italics refer to illustrations and their captions.*